GOLF

DALE CONCANNON

SUTTON PUBLISHING LIMITED

Sutton Publishing Limited
Phoenix Mill · Thrupp · Stroud
Gloucestershire · GL5 2BU

First published 1999

Copyright © Dale Concannon, 1999

British Library Cataloguing in Publication Data
A catalogue record for this book is available from the
British Library.

ISBN 0-7509-2075-0

Typeset in 10/11 Bembo.
Typesetting and origination by
Sutton Publishing Limited.
Printed in Great Britain by
Ebenezer Baylis, Worcester.

> For my Dad, Austin Concannon –
> someone whose great love of sport and history
> I have happily inherited

Allan Robertson lines up a putt at St Andrews, *c.* 1856. Photographed by Thomas Rodger, he is surrounded by some of the best known professionals of their day, including (left to right) James Wilson, William Dow, Willie Dunn, William Park, Tom Morris senior, Robertson, Daw Anderson and Bob Kirk. Asked to stand still for many minutes while the photo was taken, the weight of the clubs obviously proved too much for the caddie on the far right.

CONTENTS

Golf's first professional, Allan Robertson of St Andrews, photographed by Thomas Rodger shortly before his death in 1859.

INTRODUCTION

COLLECTING OLD GOLF PHOTOGRAPHS

It is a little known fact that no sport benefited more from the introduction of photography in the second quarter of the nineteenth century than golf.

While the Scottish town of St Andrews is widely acknowledged as the birthplace of the game, it also played host to many pioneers of early photography. In what proved a remarkable coincidence, it was somehow inevitable they would turn their attention to the Royal and Ancient game. So as those gentleman amateurs gathered on the links in the mid-1840s, together with a motley group of professionals, little could they imagine how important and indeed valuable these early images would become.

Today these first golf photographs ever taken provide an historic and revealing snapshot of the past. Offering invaluable information on the type of equipment used, the clothing worn and the courses played on, they show just how far the game of golf has come in the past 150 years. Later, as the process evolved, we are not only able to read about golfing legends of the past, but see them as well. Whether it was 'Old' Tom Morris, Harry Vardon or the immortal Bobby Jones, they offer a visual record that without a photographer there to record it, might have been lost forever.

Probably the first person ever to photograph golf and golfers was Dr John Adamson. Medical Officer for St Andrews when the town was blighted by cholera in 1848, he was a moderniser in every sense of the word. A leading member of the local Literary and Philosophical Society, not only did he found the town's first Cottage Hospital but he was also instrumental in the architectural changes deemed necessary for St Andrews' survival in the years that followed. For him, photography would prove a vital documentary tool in his study of the town and its occupants.

Inspired by Sir David Brewster, Principal of the United College, his growing interest in photography inevitably brought him into contact with golf. Having begun to experiment with different techniques from his home at 127 South Street some three years earlier, he finally took his camera out on to the links in about 1845. Gathering together a group of golfers on the rough patch of ground that served as the final green on the Old Course, Adamson posed them together as best he could.

Thankfully still in existence, this crude and blurred image reputedly shows a match between R&A stalwarts Sir Hugh Lyon Playfair and Capt. David Campbell. In the centre, the noble Lord is seen putting out while some of the game's earliest professionals, including Allan Robertson, Willie Dunn and Watty Alexander, are looking on with suitable admiration and respect. A remarkable picture, it remains the earliest sport photograph ever taken.

Golfers and caddies at St Andrews, 1850s. While top professionals Tom Morris senior (holding clubs far right) and Willie Park (third from right) were respected for their tournament play, they were still required as caddies from time to time. This photograph shows well-known R&A members Colonel J.O. Fairlie (fourth from right) and Sir Hugh Lyon Playfair (centre with top hat) playing an important club competition with their able assistance. Peering out from behind Playfair is the great Allan Robertson.

For the golfers who took part that day, the final image must have proved quite a shock: the joy of the game is certainly not evident from the severe expressions on their faces. Yet from that point on the Royal and Ancient game proved a willing subject for the photographer's lens.

After Adamson came his former laboratory assistant, Thomas Rodger. Urged by his mentor to give up his medical studies in favour of setting up the first full-time studio in St Andrews, it was from there that he photographed many of the game's early legends. From Tom Morris to winner of the first Open Championship, Willie Park, they were invariably shown holding the tools of their trade, whether it was a long nose wood or feathery golf ball.

Now considered a major figure in the history of golf photography, Rodger was also not averse to stepping out on the links to take the occasional snap. In about 1857 he took a series of photographs showing some well-known St Andrews golfers both amateur and professional. Whether this series of images was commissioned by the R&A or was merely his own fancy is unknown. Whatever the reason, the remarkable clarity of these early photographs is testimony to his own skill and technique. Taken halfway down the first fairway on the Old Course, they also offer a fascinating social insight into a bygone era. Placing them side by side, you suddenly begin to realise how the two groups never mixed!

Today these early golfing images are proving increasingly collectible. Those interested in the history and development of the game appreciate them for their documentary value, while others are continually fascinated by the complex and varied processes by which such images are attained. Whatever the reason, people are finally beginning to see golf photography as the art form it truly is.

At a recent auction of golfiana at Phillips, Edinburgh, an original Thomas Rodger photograph of the game's first professional, Allan Robertson (taken shortly before his death in 1859), sold for over £12,000. This world record price came as a real shock to collectors, who suddenly began looking at these early images in a completely different light.

Previously, most nineteenth-century golfing photographs had compared unfavourably with original artwork of the same period. Put simply, while a golf painting can be considered a one-off, there would always be a question mark over the number of prints made from a negative. Yet we now realise that many of the earliest photographs of golf were never produced in any great number – perhaps as low as four or five. But in terms of historical interest they cannot be surpassed. Unlike the artist's interpretation of a particular course or tournament, the photograph records how it really was. As if frozen in time, it captures the moment and triggers the imagination of the onlooker. That if anything is the true value of any golfing photograph.

In many cases collecting old golf photographs is all about research. Unlike an old club or ball stamped with its maker's name, photographic images invariably offer few clues regarding subject or location. Possibly the details you require were on the frame which has long since been discarded. Whatever the truth, it can prove a frustrating experience trying to work out those three vital questions – who, where and when. Indeed, this is a problem which can apply as much to photographs from the 1950s as those from the 1850s.

Ben Sayers contemplating a difficult bunker shot at North Berwick in 1896.

Invariably identification is often the key to a good collection, because the simple truth is that one golfer with a moustache can look very much like another in that old photograph you own. And while Open Champions from the turn of the century like Vardon, Braid and Taylor are easily recognisable, it is surprising just how many white-bearded gentlemen have been wrongly credited as 'Old' Tom Morris in the past.

For the experienced collector, the most difficult of all nineteenth-century images to identify is the group photograph. This is where members of a club or society would get together during a competition and have their picture taken for posterity. With practice, dating the photo from the clothing and clubs on display is simple enough. You might even be fortunate enough to read the inscription on the actual trophy with the aid of a magnifying glass. Yet without a famous face to go on they will probably always remain an anonymous group of golfers. Of course, if it was taken at either St Andrews, North Berwick or Carnoustie, it becomes a relatively simple piece of detective work tracking down the societies that played there at any given time. That is where the research comes in.

Having said that, golf courses can also provide the occasional headache when it comes to identification – especially when dealing with individual holes. With the marked exception of the Old Course at St Andrews, which has changed little over the past one hundred years, one golf hole can look very much like another without a discernible landmark in the background. It is also likely that many courses have undergone extensive renovations over the past few decades. For example, it is a little-known fact that Muirfield began with a short par 3 back in the 1890s and not the long par 4 hole which it currently has!

On the positive side, there are still countless thousands of golfing photographs left to collect. While the earliest Scottish images remain rare and difficult to find, modern-day antique fairs often sell albums full of Edwardian snaps which often include golf. Alternatively the period from 1920 to 1950 can also offer some wonderful opportunities to build a fine collection; many of the larger, more professional images will inevitably carry the stamp of the photographic agency who commissioned it. Who would not want to own an original photo of Walter Hagen, Gene Sarazen or Ben Hogan?

Failing that, there are always golfing magazines or books. While not originals, they provide an insight into just how long golf photography has been around. At the turn of the century publications like *Golf Illustrated* relied on the latest photographs of Harry Vardon to help sell their product much like Tiger Woods today. A few years earlier, in 1887, Sir Walter Simpson boasted about the 'instantaneous' photographs used to illustrate his book *The Art of Golf*: today we take it for granted that the books and magazines we read will be adorned with colourful images of golf and golfers, and it is difficult to imagine what a proud claim this really was, back then.

So as you leaf through the pages of this book remember all those people who loved the game enough to take photographs of it. Taken from my own collection, each one has been carefully selected for its historical significance, individual charm and, in some cases, downright curiosity. Many have never been published before while others are classic images from golf's past. I hope you find as much pleasure in looking at them as I had collecting them.

Good Golfing.

Dale Concannon
England

CHAPTER ONE

ST ANDREWS & SCOTLAND: THE HOME OF GOLF

Golf has a history stretching back over five hundred years. While its exact origins are unknown, it was popular enough to be banned throughout Scotland in 1457 because it interfered with compulsory archery practice. Since that dark hour the Royal and Ancient game has spread well beyond Scottish shores to take root in almost every country in the world. Yet wherever golf is played the small east coast town of St Andrews will always remain its spiritual home.

All the legends of golf have played here, from 'Young' Tom Morris to Harry Vardon, Walter Hagen to Ben Hogan, Arnold Palmer to Jack Nicklaus; there is no other place on earth where golf history comes alive like St Andrews. Mary, Queen of Scots, a frequent visitor to the links in her youth, once described St Andrews as, 'the most pleasing town in my kingdom'. Today there are countless thousands of golfing pilgrims who visit the 'Old Grey Toon' each year who would certainly agree with her.

Home to the Open Championship and countless other international events, the Old Course has changed little since it was formed centuries ago. Occupying a narrow finger of land between St Andrews Bay and the Eden estuary, it stretches away from the town like a shepherd's crook. Yet at first sight it appears flat and uninspiring, with little of the colour and majestic splendour of Pebble Beach or Augusta National. The first time American professional Sam Snead saw it through the window of his railway carriage, he thought the starkly primitive course was abandoned!

Indeed, the majority of fairways at St Andrews do resemble a moonscape and rarely, if ever, offer the golfer a flat lie to play his shot. Benign when the sun shines, a monster when the wind blows, the Old Course is also the most fiendishly bunkered golf links in the world. As if getting out of them was not difficult enough, they all have evocative names like 'Coffins', 'Lions Mouth', 'Grave' and, perhaps most intimidating of all, 'Hell'.

Another future Open champion who initially found the ancient links not to his liking was Bobby Jones. Making his debut there in 1921, he tore up his scorecard in disgust after failing to escape from Strath bunker on the eleventh in the third round. Storming off the course, he swore never to return. Yet, like Snead, Jones would return – to win the second of his three Open titles there in 1927. Years later he wrote: 'If I had to play one golf course for the rest of my life it would be the Old Course at St Andrews.'

St Andrews is also home to the Royal and Ancient Golf Club. Yet with golf thought to have been played on the links for over five centuries, the R&A is perhaps not quite as 'ancient' as its title suggests. The original club was formed in 1754 by 'twenty-two noblemen and gentlemen being admirers of the ancient and healthful exercise of the Golf'. Taking a lead from the Honourable Company who played at Leith, they raised enough money to provide a silver club as a competition prize. Drafting some rules on to those already provided, the Society of St Andrews Golfers took to the links for their first competition the same year, and have been playing there ever since.

Back then the Old Course was made up of twenty-two holes. With the narrow strip of land only wide enough for one fairway and one green, a typical round consisted of playing eleven holes out, then the same again in reverse. Of course, using the same green twice meant the chance of injury from an errant feathery ball was fairly commonplace, until someone had the bright idea of widening the greens and splitting the fairways. Even then there were strong complaints in 1764 after William St Clair went round the links in the sacrilegious score of 121 strokes!

Golf had become too easy, they said, and the course was promptly reduced to a much tougher eighteen holes – the standard by which all courses are now set. A few decades later the Society of St Andrews Golfers also stole a march on their Edinburgh rivals by applying to King William IV for royal patronage. Two years later, in 1837, it was finally agreed, with the newly titled 'Royal and Ancient Golf Club' naming a medal after the Sovereign in grateful thanks for the honour bestowed upon them.

Gradually, with a permanent and more prestigious home needed, the present clubhouse was built at the head of the Old Course in 1854. From there the R&A quietly established itself at the very centre of golf in Scotland, with all other clubs deferring to them on the matter of the rules. Today the club is acknowledged as the centre of rule making, along with the United States Golf Association.

Apart from legislating on the rules of golf, perhaps the most important function of the R&A is its supervision of the Open Championship. Totally independent from the Professional Golfers Association and European Tour, it has administered this most famous event for over one hundred years.

Over the years the town of St Andrews has also produced its fair share of legendary golfers and Open Champions, with the most famous being 'Old' and 'Young' Tom Morris. Regarded somewhat as an elder statesman by the time he died in 1908, Tom Morris senior probably saw more golf history – and created more – than any other professional ever connected with the game. During his eight decades in the game he was a respected tournament player, caddie, lay preacher, ball maker and golf course architect. And if this was not enough, he raised eight children, one of whom went on to become the greatest golfer in the world.

Born in St Andrews, Morris was apprenticed in his younger years to another great champion, Allan Robertson. A feather ball maker by trade, he was the only player to break 80 over the Old Course and was openly acknowledged as Scotland's finest player. Later partnering Tom Morris to many of his greatest challenge match victories, especially over the Park's and the Dunn's, Robertson himself was considered almost unbeatable in head-to-head singles play.

Robertson eventually fell victim to jaundice in 1859, still playing at the peak of his form in the months before, when the question had arisen about who was the best golfer in Scotland – Robertson or Morris? With the first Open Championship scheduled for Prestwick one year later, that question might have been finally answered. But whatever the outcome it is likely that Morris would not have won all four of his titles if his old mentor had been around to compete in those early championships. Yet as skilled as Robertson obviously was, this would certainly not have been the case with his son Tom Morris junior.

In many people's opinion, Young Tom was a golfing genius. Born in Prestwick, where his father held the post of Keeper of the Greens for twelve years from 1851, he was a confident player with a sure touch on the greens (unlike 'Old' Tom, who once received a letter addressed to the 'misser of short putts, Prestwick!')

Winning his first Open title at 17, Tommie became the first golfer in history to win three consecutive championships in 1868–69–70. Having been presented with the challenge belt, he was then forced to wait until 1872 to win his fourth title; the silver claret jug was not available, so the tournament was cancelled.

Returning to St Andrews with his father, Tommie rarely shunned the opportunity to play for money. In May 1874 he played the best ball of professional Watty MacDonald and two others, and won by 2&1. A week later he and his good friend Davie Strath beat MacDonald and four others by an even greater margin! With little concern for the odds, he once bet that he could shoot 83 or better every day for a week on the Old Course – and did. And this in the days when top amateurs were winning competitions with scores of 95 or more. . . .

As his fame grew apace, so did the growing number of golfers in Scotland. While the typical golf professional still had little standing in society, Open tournaments like those held at Perth, Aberdeen and of course Prestwick in the west, were proving increasingly popular – not least because they offered a good opportunity for the upper classes to bet money on the outcome.

Sadly, though, the story of Young Tom Morris has a tragic ending. Having partnered his father to victory over Willie and Mungo Park at North Berwick in September 1875, news came through that his wife was seriously ill while in childbirth. Since no train was at hand, a local member offered to sail both men across the Firth of Forth to St Andrews in his yacht.

Arriving at the harbour, the party was met by the Morris family doctor, who informed Young Tom that both mother and baby had died. Stricken by the news, he took little interest in anything in the coming weeks, least of all his health. While he was persuaded to play one last match against Arthur Molesworth, a noted amateur from Royal North Devon, the damage caused by playing three rounds in biting cold conditions weakened him even further. Shortly afterwards he died of a pulmonary embolism on Christmas morning 1875.

In his memory sixty golfing societies from Scotland and England contributed to the erection of a permanent memorial in the cemetery at St Andrews Cathedral. Today, like the town itself, it remains a place of pilgrimage for golfers everywhere. As does Scotland, the true home of golf.

Hugh Philp of St Andrews. Born in 1782 at Cameron, Fife, he established a unique reputation for making long-nose woods from 1810 to 1856. Known for his wonderful putters, he was said to have polished them countless times to obtain the exact finish he required. He was later appointed official club maker of the Society of St Andrews Golfers (later the Royal and Ancient) in 1819. His early clubs are extremely collectible, with their value often measured in thousands of pounds.

A very special antique putter from the early 1850s. Not only is this long-nose club the work of master club maker Hugh Philp, it is stamped with the names of two early professionals, George Daniel Brown and William Dow. Owned by both men in turn, it is almost certain that this club was used in the very first Open Championship at Prestwick in 1860: a real treasure.

Golfers playing to the first green at St Andrews, *c.* 1850. The opening green on the Old Course was situated where the Road hole green (17th) is today.

Professionals and amateurs gather outside the Royal and Ancient's new clubhouse prior to the Grand Tournament of 1857. Completed only three years earlier, it remained primarily a single storey building up until 1878 when an upper floor was added.

Hay Erskine Wemyss, captain of the R&A in 1854, prepares to drive off the first at St Andrews. One of the earliest known photographs of Scottish golf, it dates from around 1857 and includes both Tom Morris senior (far left) and Allan Robertson (third from the right). It also shows that there were no golf bags available to the caddie. The clubs were tucked under the arm as shown by Bob Kirk in the centre.

A group of early Scottish professionals photographed at St Andrews by Thomas Rodger, *c.* 1857. In the centre holding a club over his shoulder is Allan Robertson. The first golfer to break 80 over the Old Course, he was acknowledged as the finest golfer of his era. Immediately to his left wearing a dark jacket is the legendary Tom Morris senior. Great rivals until Robertson's untimely death from jaundice two years later, Morris actually began his professional life as his assistant, learning how to make feathery balls.

An early photograph of St Andrews golf. Robert Chambers is seen here holing his final putt to win the 1858 Matchplay Tournament at St Andrews. To his right is Sir Hugh Lyon Playfair (kneeling and wearing top hat) and seated in the background is the famous caddie 'Long Willie'. The photograph was no doubt taken at a later date to commemorate Chambers' famous victory. Each individual would have been forced to stand still for many minutes while the image was allowed to develop.

A jacketed golfer negotiates his way out of a fearsome hazard on the Old Course in 1858.

Tom Morris senior and Tom Morris junior dominated the early years of the Open Championship. From 1861 to 1874 this legendary father and son partnership shared eight titles between them. The portrait was taken shortly before 'Young' Tom's premature death in 1875, and he was known to have liked it above all others. Therefore it came as no surprise that when a suitable monument was sought for his grave in St Andrews Cathedral this image was chosen. Sixty or more golf societies from all over Britain contributed to its cost. Today it remains a place of pilgrimage for golfers all over the world.

The legendary 'Old' Tom Morris of St Andrews.

Tom Morris junior (1851–75). A brilliant but ultimately tragic figure, he won four consecutive Open titles, the last when he was just 21. Pictured wearing his beloved champion's belt, he would be dead within a year of this photograph being taken.

Golfers playing out of Hell bunker at St Andrews, *c.* 1865.

An early golfing scene at St Andrews, *c.* 1880. Unlike today, golfers drove off within one club length of the hole using sand scooped out of the bottom on which to tee the ball, leaving the green a sorry mess to putt on. It would be another decade before separate tee-ing areas were introduced.

A rare photograph of Bob Martin, winner of the Open Championship at St Andrews in 1885.

The British Amateur Championship trophy. First played for in 1887 at Hoylake, the engraved silver cup with the figure of 'Old' Tom Morris standing on top remains perhaps the most attractive of all the major trophies.

Robert Forgan's workshop at St Andrews, *c.* 1890. One of the most respected clubmakers in Scotland, Forgan was among the first to export wooden shafted clubs overseas to India, Australia and the United States. Taking clubmaking away from the single craftsman and into the age of mass-production, up to seventy staff were employed during the company's golden era between 1890 to 1915. The photograph above shows the finishing shop, where wooden heads were smoothed over with a fine plane before being fitted with a hickory shaft.

A rare and unusual photograph showing the workforce at Forgan & Sons of St Andrews. While group photographs of this kind are not uncommon, this one dating from 1895 shows the workers actually holding the tools of their trade. Robert Forgan himself is seated in the centre with the long white beard, while his staff exhibit the chisels, saws and raw materials used in club and ball making during the period.

'Old' Tom Morris – Open Champion, ball and club maker, golf course architect and probably St Andrews' favourite son.

James Mentiply, Works Foreman of Forgan and Sons, St Andrews, demonstrates how it took a top hat full of goose feathers to fill one old feathery golf ball in 1925.

Two feather-filled golf balls, *c.* 1840. They are about the same size and weight of a modern golf ball. The longest drive with a 'feathery' is well over 300 yards!

Willie Auchterlonie, winner of the Open Championship in 1893. Born in St Andrews, and apprenticed as a club maker at nearby Forgan's, he is believed to have been the only professional ever to have won the Open with clubs he made himself!

Frederick Guthrie Tait pictured at his beloved St Andrews, 1895. A superb young player, he won the Amateur Championship in 1896 and 1898 and was runner-up in 1899. He also finished third in the Open Championship on two occasions. Sadly in 1900 he was killed in action at Koodoosberg Drift while leading his company of the Black Watch in the Boer War, a loss felt most strongly in his home town. The R&A immediately commissioned a portrait of him for the clubhouse. It remains there to this day.

Arthur Balfour MP driving himself in as captain of the Royal and Ancient, 1894, a few short years before he became British Prime Minister. 'Old' Tom Morris can be seen applauding enthusiastically in the background.

'Old' Tom Morris enjoying a refreshing glass of ginger beer at St Andrews in 1895. Run for many years by ex-caddie Daw Anderson, the stall became such a familiar part of the Old Course that author Robert Clark mentioned it in a poem: 'A pot of beer! Go dip thine angry beak in it, and straight its rage shall melt to soft placidity.' Today the actual hole where it was sold – the fourth – is aptly named the 'Ginger Beer' hole.

'Old' Tom Morris tends the flagstick on the final green during the Autumn Medal at St Andrews, 1896. Note the children standing in the background. Almost certainly boy caddies, some are watching the action bare-footed.

The first tee at St Andrews, 1898. Note how far forward the tee is down the fairway compared with today.

Large crowds gather on the first tee at St Andrews to watch a challenge match between professionals, including Alex Herd and Andrew Kirkaldy. A not uncommon sight in the late 1890s, 'Old' Tom Morris can be seen in the background acting as official starter.

Golfers on the second hole at St Andrews in 1896. Note the rather shabby condition of the tee before the days of automatic sprinklers!

The first motor car arrives in St Andrews in 1905: it was owned by James Wilson, a local businessman who later established the first garage in South Street. The photograph shows Tom Morris sitting in the passenger seat. As you can see from the large crowds gathered near Granny Clarks Wynd, this was a big occasion in the history of the town.

The Auchterlonie golf shop – perhaps the most recognisable name in St Andrews golf, photographed here in the '20s. The sign on the left reads: 'Tom Auchterlonie – Maker of superior hand made golf clubs of every description. Repairs of all kinds promptly executed by skilled club makers.'

Edward, Prince of Wales drives himself in as captain of the Royal and Ancient Golf Club in 1922. The shot by all accounts was a low top.

Large crowds gather around the fourteenth hole during the morning round of Bobby Jones' thirty-six hole British Amateur final against Roger Wethered at St Andrews, 1930.

Stylish English amateur Roger Wethered takes on Bobby Jones in the final of the British Amateur Championship at St Andrews, 1930.

With Bobby Jones having defeated Roger Wethered in the final of the 1930 British Amateur at St Andrews, the crowds rush forward to the final green to get a glimpse of the presentation.

Having just won the 1930 British Amateur Championship at St Andrews, American star Bobby Jones is escorted through the excited crowds by two burly policemen.

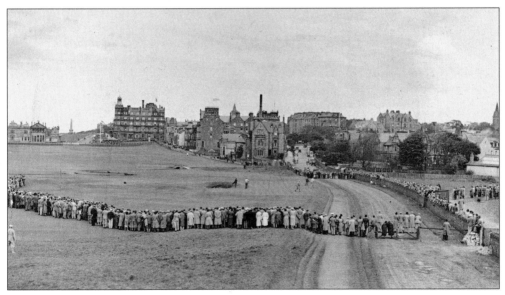

Little has changed over the past few hundred years. This photograph shows the Old Course at St Andrews in the late 1940s.

Legendary Bruntsfield caddie 'Big' Harry
Crawford. Like most caddies around the turn
of the century, he was poorly educated and not
averse to a drop of the hard stuff. Yet in later
life he gained a degree of respectability by
running a ginger beer stall near the first tee at
North Berwick.

A rare photograph of golfers at Bruntsfield in Edinburgh, *c.* 1855. Caddies include Tom Morris senior
(second from the right) and Watty Alexander (far left).

An important group photograph of early Scottish professionals. Taken in Perth in about 1864, it includes (left to right) William Park, James Johnstone, Tom Morris junior (as a young boy), Tom Morris senior, George Daniel Brown, David Park, William Dow, Charles Hunter, Robert Andrews, Andrew Strath (in front holding club) and Watty MacDonald (in front).

Two well-dressed children playing golf on the streets of Edinburgh, *c.* 1869.

St Andrews Golf Club versus Forfarshire at Monifieth, 19 June 1897. Still in existence today, the St Andrews club can boast more major winning champions than any other private club in golf. Pictured in this early photograph is 1902 US Open winner Laurie Auchterlonie (back row, second from the right) and 1898 US Open champion Fred Herd (sitting directly in front of him). While he never won anything of significance, Andrew Greig (lying down in the foreground) became official starter on the Old Course in around 1910. A brusque character, he was approached by a Monsieur Fouquier about his tee-off time. 'Well,' said Greig, showing little interest in writing out the Frenchman's name in his visitors book, 'When I cry out Mr Tamson you just step on to that tee yonder.'

An unnamed golf society, 1880. From the golfers' clothing, outdated wooden-headed clubs and rough canvas sheet used as a background, this is not a wealthy group and it must have stretched their finances to have this photograph taken. Quite what part the carriage whip plays in proceedings is left to the imagination.

The rugged links of North Berwick, *c.* 1885. While rated among the finest courses in Scotland, it was surprisingly never selected as the venue for the Open Championship.

Willie Park junior versus Harry Vardon at North Berwick, 1899. One of the most eagerly anticipated challenge matches of the year, it was played over two rounds at Ganton and North Berwick for £100, and attracted large crowds at both venues. Reigning Open champion Vardon eventually won by the large margin of 11&10.

Caddie boys at Prestwick, 1898.

'The Great International Foursome' of 1905. English professionals Harry Vardon (seated right) and J.H. Taylor (standing right) played Scotland, represented by James Braid (seated left) and Alex Herd (standing right) over two rounds at St Andrews, Troon, Deal and St Anne's. Watched by thousands, England finally ran out winners by 13 up and 12 to play.

CHAPTER TWO

THE OLDEST OPEN
OF ALL

The first Open Championship was held on 17 October 1860 at Prestwick Golf Club on the west coast of Scotland. Compared with the vast international sporting event it has since become, this was a relatively modest affair with only eight competitors and no prize money. Although not truly 'open' until the following year, when amateurs were allowed to compete alongside the professionals, it is simply known throughout the golfing world as *the* Open Championship.

Designed to find the 'Champion Golfer of Scotland', the tournament had been proposed as early as 1855. Prestwick, perhaps feeling they were not established enough to hold such an important event, originally approached the Royal and Ancient Golf Club at St Andrews in the hope they might stage it. After much procrastination the idea was eventually turned down, so they asked Musselburgh, but once again there seemed little interest.

Frustrated at the long delay, the members at Prestwick eventually decided to go it alone and donated funds from which a silver challenge belt was bought. Made from morocco red leather and with a silver buckle, it was modelled on a typical prize fighting belt of the time and cost the not insubstantial sum of 30 guineas. Offered as the prize to any golfer who won the tournament three times, invitations were sent out to every golf club in Scotland to enter their champion – including St Andrews and Musselburgh.

Unlike today, organised events like the one arranged at Prestwick were not particularly popular with the professionals themselves. With the exception of Tom Morris senior, who had taken up the well-paid post of Keeper of the Greens at the Ayrshire club in 1851, the majority scratched a living by caddying or giving the odd lesson. Often living from hand to mouth, they would also take part in the occasional challenge match where large sums were often wagered on the outcome, and took a percentage in expenses. Perhaps this explains why there were only eight entrants in a tournament with no prize money on offer.

Played over three rounds of the twelve hole course, the first Open Championship was won by William Park senior of Musselburgh, beating the local favourite, Tom Morris, into second. The quality of Park's play had impressed everyone including the lone reporter from the *Ayr Advertiser*, who wrote: 'We have no hesitation in saying, that at times the game of golf was never seen in such great perfection. . . .'

Despite having to bail one of the competitors from a local jail the night before the tournament, Prestwick appeared delighted with the way the event had been received. After presenting the silver belt to Park, the club announced that from the following year the tournament would be 'open to the world!', which in this particular case meant gentleman amateurs. Yet in the first twelve years of the championship – all held at Prestwick – the amateurs of Scotland made little impact on the competition.

With entries still only ranging between eight and seventeen, Willie Park won again in 1863, but the event itself came to be dominated by the father and son combination of Tom Morris senior and Tom Morris junior. Capturing eight titles between them, there is no doubt that it was their popularity alone which kept interest in the tournament alive in those early years.

After his three consecutive victories in 1868, '69 and '70 'Young' Tom was given permanent possession of the silver challenge belt, forcing Prestwick to supply another trophy for the tournament – the famed silver claret jug. Both St Andrews and Musselburgh were invited to contribute toward the cost. This was agreed on the understanding that the event would alternate between the three clubs, and the Open rota which still exists today was born.

In the coming decades the Open Championship continued to grow in stature. As the original home of the Honourable Company of Edinburgh Golfers, Musselburgh became 'disagreeably overcrowded' when their new course at Muirfield was included in the list. Two years later, in 1894, Royal St George's at Sandwich became the first English course to stage the tournament. From that point on the Open became truly British, with other prestigious venues like Royal Liverpool, Deal, Troon, Royal Lytham, Carnoustie, Royal Portrush and Royal Birkdale gradually being introduced.

After the death of Tom Morris junior in 1875 at the young age of 24, the tournament itself became a little more open. While 'Old' Tom would not add to his tally of four championship victories, Willie Park senior had returned to pick up his third title earlier the same year. In 1876 the event saw its first major controversy, when David Strath refused a play-off with Bob Martin after seeing his ball kicked away by his supporters on the famed road hole at St Andrews during normal play. Somewhat tainted by the incident, the Open desperately needed a new hero, and one year later two duly arrived in the shape of Jamie Anderson and Bob Ferguson.

The competition between these two professionals, who shared the next six championships between them, excited interest in the event when perhaps it was waning slightly. Born in St Andrews, Jamie Anderson was a close friend of 'Young' Tom and partnered him on many challenge matches. Reputedly a long hitter of the new gutta-percha ball, he won the Open three times in a row from 1877. Ferguson, who then picked up where he left off by winning the Open in 1880, 1881 and 1882, was an older man from Musselburgh who made his living mainly as a caddy. Yet in some ways both are the forgotten men of Open Championship history, who deserve far more credit.

Both professionals won their three titles on three different courses, unlike Tom Morris junior who won his four over his 'home' links of Prestwick. Also, while Anderson and Ferguson received prize money for their efforts – something introduced in 1871 – neither professional actually got to keep the trophy for good. (A clause was brought in after 'Young' Tom's third win in 1870 had left the Open with no trophy to play for!)

The following decade brought a selection of new champions, and not all of them professionals. In 1890 John Ball junior from Royal Liverpool pushed past Champion Willie Fernie into second place at Prestwick. Two years later at Muirfield it was an amateur one-two, as Ball finished runner-up to Harold Hilton. They were fellow members at Hoylake, and it would be the first of Hilton's two titles before eventually moving on to become editor of *Golf Monthly* magazine.

With the Scottish stranglehold on the Open Championship now truly broken, the way was paved for a new era in the history of the championship – that of the 'Great Triumvirate'. Today it is difficult to imagine three golfers dominating the tournament for over two decades as these men did. But in the twenty-one years from 1894 to the outbreak of the First World War Harry Vardon, James Braid and John Henry Taylor won the title no fewer than sixteen times between them.

J.H. Taylor was the first English professional to win the Open, in 1894 at Sandwich, and the first of the Triumvirate to make a showing. Born within chipping distance of Royal North Devon Golf Club in 1871, the son of a working-class labourer, Taylor was a remarkable character who not only taught himself how to read and write but play golf as well. A doughty competitor, he was a scratch golfer by the age of 17 and funded his early career by working as

A group of early Scottish professionals gather for the Grand Golf Tournament at Leith Links, May 1857. Looking ill at ease with the camera, they were mostly poorly educated caddies who lived from hand to mouth for most of the year. From left to right: Andrew Strath, David Park, Bob Kirk, James Anderson, James Dunn, William Dow, William Dunn, Andrew Greig, Tom Morris senior, Tom Morris junior and George Morris.

a green keeper at the club. Later establishing a highly successful club making business, he won five Open titles as well as countless other professional events.

James Braid was born in 1870 at Earlsferry near St Andrews. At 6 feet 2 inches, he was a tall gangling figure with a whiplash swing, who had the reputation of being a long, but not always straight, driver of the ball. A late bloomer in professional terms, he literally monopolised the Open in the early 1900s. Starting with his unexpected victory at Muirfield in 1901 – where he beat Vardon into second place – he won the title four more times in the next nine years. It might have been even more, had Braid not suffered from bouts of severe motion sickness which prevented him travelling over to America for the US Open with Taylor and Vardon.

Later appointed professional at Walton Heath Golf Club in Surrey, Braid remained a highly respected player with a strong following in his home country – no doubt helped by the fact that he won four of his five titles in Scotland! Not only that, he took great pleasure in taking on the 'auld enemy' in the popular international foursomes matches, which matched him against the 'English' team of Vardon and Taylor, usually partnered by 1903 Open champion Alex Herd. These were always close affairs which thrilled the golfing public and helped promote the game more widely.

Of the Great Triumvirate, Harry Vardon is perhaps the best known of the three professionals. Born in Jersey in 1870, he won the Open Championship a record six times despite being dogged by ill health and the dreaded putting yips throughout most of his life. Nicknamed the 'Greyhound' by his fellow professional Andra Kirkaldy, because of the way he came through to win so many tournaments in the closing stages, Vardon was essentially a shy man. A smooth swinger with a nerveless temperament, he was certainly the most gifted of the three.

In 1896 he followed Taylor's second Open win at St Andrews with one of his own at Muirfield. Adding to his total in 1899, 1903, 1911 and 1914, he also became the first player in history to achieve the Open double when he relegated Taylor into second place in the US Open in Chicago in 1900. The greatest golfer of his generation, his career was cruelly cut short by the advent of war in 1914. When the championship resumed in 1920 at Deal, he showed what might have been by finishing tied fourteenth behind winner George Duncan at the age of fifty.

After the war it soon became obvious that the balance of power had shifted from Britain to the United States. In 1921 Jock Hutchison edged out the elegant English amateur Roger Wethered in a play-off, to win the first Open held at St Andrews for over a decade. While Hutchison was born in the 'auld grey toon' he had taken up American citizenship some years before. It was the same with Tommy Armour, winner at Carnoustie in 1931, Scottish born and bred but a naturalised American. It would sadly be the closest Scotland would come to having a home-grown champion for over half a century.

The remaining history of the Open Championship can be split into four neat piles. Throughout most of the '20s and early '30s the event was dominated by two legendary Americans, Walter Hagen and Robert T. Jones junior. Sharing seven Open titles between them – four and three respectively – they took the game of golf to a new level. Along with them, Gene Sarazen, Jim Barnes and Denny Shute all added to the US domination of the event, with one victory each.

The second period takes in the time immediately before and after the Second World War. Known as the 'Commonwealth' era, it began with Henry Cotton's victory at Sandwich in 1933. The first of his three Open titles, it rejuvenated British interest in the event and inspired further 'home' wins by Alf Perry, Alf Padgham, Reg Whitcome and Dick Burton. After the war Fred Daly became the first Irish professional to win the title, while Max Faulkner came through to win the only event held outside the British mainland, at Royal Portrush in 1951.

While top Americans, with the exception of Sam Snead (winner in 1946) and Ben Hogan (1953), were no longer competing, those players from the old Commonwealth countries certainly were. Led by Bobby Locke of South Africa, winner in 1949 and 1950, and five-time champion Peter Thompson from Australia, the Open saw other wins from Kel Nagle (Australia), Gary Player (South Africa) and Bob Charles (New Zealand). The event was now a truly international affair, and it was not long before the United States showed a more sustained interest.

In 1961 Arnold Palmer won the first of his two Open titles at Royal Birkdale. Both charismatic and powerful, his play throughout the early 1960s inspired a new generation of American golfers to compete in the Open. Following hard on his heels was the great Jack Nicklaus, who was slightly younger. Theirs was a rivalry that stretched across the Atlantic to encompass every major championship, including the Open.

From then until the late 1970s professionals from the United States resumed their dominance of golf's oldest championship. In a twenty-year period the silver claret jug has witnessed more American names than at any previous time, including Tony Lema, Lee Trevino, Tom Weiskopf, Johnny Miller and five-time winner Tom Watson. With the notable exception of Englishman Tony Jacklin in 1969, no home-grown player managed to loosen their stranglehold on the trophy.

Today it seems little has changed. Apart from a sparkling period in the '80s and early '90s when Europeans Severiano Ballesteros, Sandy Lyle and Nick Faldo won seven titles between them, the pendulum now appears to have swung back in favour of the USA. With John Daly, Tom Lehmann, Justin Leonard and Mark O'Meara all winning in the '90s who can tell? Perhaps that is what makes 'the Oldest Open of all' so fascinating.

'Old' Tom Morris is one of the most legendary figures in the game of golf. During his eight decades, he probably saw more golf history – and created more – than any other player connected with the Royal and Ancient game. He was in turn an apprentice feather ball maker, a caddie, a legendary tournament player, a golf course designer and if that was not enough, father to the greatest golfer of his generation – 'Young' Tom Morris junior. Born in 1821, 'Old' Tom was appointed 'Keeper of the Greens' at the newly formed Prestwick Golf Club in 1851. It was there, ten years later, that he won his first Open at the relatively advanced age of 40. Having finished runner-up to his long-time rival Willie Park in the first ever championship held the year before, he triumphed again in 1862, 1864 and 1867, and is forever synonymous with the ancient Scottish town of St Andrews. The Royal and Ancient clubhouse today bears a commemorative plaque looking down on the first tee.

This is possibly the first ever photograph taken at the Open Golf Championship, Prestwick, *c.* 1860. The two golfers standing in the foreground are Charlie Hunter (left) and Tom Morris senior (putting). Like the other competitors, they are dressed in tartan jackets given to them by club patron the Earl of Eglington. Because many of the professionals arrived for the event so badly attired, the Club became concerned about what any female visitors would think – hence the jackets!

A studio portrait of Willie Park senior of Musselburgh, *c.* 1863. The winner of the first Open Championship held at Prestwick in 1860, he rarely played non competitive matches and even advertised in *Bell's Life* magazine offering to play anyone for £100 – amateur or professional!

Willie Park, winner of the first Open Championship in 1860, photographed in old age. Unlike his great rival Tom Morris, Park never built on his great reputation as a player and returned in later life to making clubs at Musselburgh. Eventually retiring in 1890, he died thirteen years later aged 69.

Tom Morris junior wearing the original Open champion belt, photographed by Thomas Rodger of St Andrews shortly after the belt was presented to him by the Prestwick Golf Club as the prize for winning his third consecutive title in 1870. He returned two years later to capture the fourth and last Open Championship at the same course. Yet shortly after winning again in 1872, his life came to a tragic end. In 1875 his wife Elizabeth died while giving birth to their first child. Having received the news during a challenge match at North Berwick, he neglected his own health over the following months and died in St Andrews on Christmas Day 1875. He was only 24.

Winner of the 1874 Open at Musselburgh, Mungo Park, Brother of Willie Park, winner of the first Open in 1860.

A rare studio photograph of David Strath, c. 1864. A strong rival to Tom Morris junior, he is associated with one of the most unusual finishes in Open championship history. At St Andrews in 1876 he was tied with Bob Martin for the title but refused to take part in the play-off after accusing his rival's supporters of kicking the ball back into play on the penultimate hole! Sadly, he was to die three years later during a long sea voyage to Australia.

Willie Fernie, winner of the 1883 Open Championship. A plasterer by trade, he defeated odds-on favourite Bob Ferguson in a mammoth thirty-six hole play-off at Musselburgh to record his first and only title. On the strength of his win, Fernie gave up his club post at Dumfries for a better paid one at Felixstowe in England. Finally ending up at Troon, he is perhaps best known for having designed the Ailsa course at Turnberry.

The gold Open medal presented to Jack Simpson for his victory at Prestwick in 1884.

Golfers at Prestwick, *c.* 1889, the home of the first Open Golf Championship in 1860. 'Old' Tom Morris (centre) finished runner-up there to his great rival from Musselburgh, William Park.

The original Open Championship belt presented to the winner between 1860 and 1870.

John Carey of Musselburgh was a famous caddie in the late 1890s. His nickname 'Fiery' stemmed not from his temperament but from his ruddy complexion. Known to be a quiet, private figure, his advice was only given when asked for. The regular caddie of Willie Park junior in all his Open Championship triumphs and big money challenge matches, he always wore his trademark Balmoral bonnet. Having begun caddying before the advent of the leather golf bag, Fiery continued to hold the clubs underarm long after the bag strap had made such a style obsolete.

Portrait of two-time Open winner, Willie Park junior. A highly intelligent individual, he not only became a golfing champion, but also a successful businessman, author, club designer and golf course architect.

An early photograph of John Ball junior, winner of the 1890 Open at Prestwick. The first ever amateur to win the title, he was a relatively shy man who failed to capitalise on his great fame. A member at Royal Liverpool along with his great rival, Harold Hilton, he was recognised as the supreme match player, winning a record eight British Amateur titles before his death in 1940. Later asked to loan his impressive collection of medals for an exhibition in London, Ball was forced to decline – saying he had given most of them away to friends.

Hugh Kirkaldy, wearing his 1891 Open winners medal. The lesser known of two brothers from St Andrews, he pushed Andra' into second place alongside Willie Fernie.

Open Golf Championship at Muirfield, 1896. John Henry Taylor is shown teeing off against Harry Vardon in the first hole of a play-off for the title. While Vardon would eventually run out the winner, it is interesting to note that the short hole they are playing across the front of the clubhouse no longer exists. Today the only course on the Open rotation which starts with an opening par 3 is Royal Lytham and St Anne's.

Harry Vardon putting on the final green at Muirfield during the 1896 Open Championship. Going on to beat J.H. Taylor in a play-off for the title, the photograph shows the relaxed way spectators viewed the golf at the time. It is also interesting to see how many women were present at a time when they would have been barred from playing the course themselves.

Harry Vardon (in the white jacket) putting out on the 'Alps' green at Prestwick on his way to winning the Open, 1898. What makes this photo interesting is that it was found in the attic of Vardon's own house in Totteridge almost fifty years after his death in 1937.

Six-time Open Champion Harry Vardon in his prime. When renowned British artist Clement Fowler was commissioned to paint his 1913 portrait of the 'Great Triumvirate' he failed to persuade Vardon to make enough time for a sitting. Instead, he selected this 1893 photograph for his painting, aging the face a little!

Harry Vardon, six-time British Open Champion, clearly showing the grip named after him.

Six-time Open Champion Harry Vardon.
Consistently plagued by ill health throughout his
career, even having a spell in a sanatorium in
Norfolk, he became the most respected golfer of
his era. Later nicknamed the 'Greyhound' by his
fellow professional Andrew Kirkaldy, because of
his ability to race through in the final stages of a
tournament, his all-round game had no peer.
Taken in 1920, this photograph is among the
best ever portraits of this private man.

Harry Vardon in relaxed mood at the age of 55. No
longer competing in major championships like the
Open, he contented himself by playing the odd
exhibition match and running his professional shop
at Totteridge Golf Club, north of London.

James Braid, five-time Open Champion.
Compared with his great rivals, Harry Vardon
and J.H. Taylor, this tall, elegant Scot came
late to championship golf. But having
captured his first Open title in 1901 at the
relatively advanced age of 31, he just kept on
winning. Joining the other two as the third
member of the so-called 'Great Triumvirate,'
he won four more championships over the
next nine years.

James Braid driving off at North Berwick,
1904. Considered a long hitter, he was
increasingly hampered in old age by poor
eyesight, caused by having lime accidentally
thrown into his eyes as a youth. His vision was
so bad in 1913 that he was advised not to play
in the Open. Braid disregarded the advice, put
on dark glasses and played on without
complaint.

The well-known St Andrews firm of David and William Auchterlonie exhibiting their latest golf equipment at the Open Championship in 1910. Because the grips were made of best calf leather, it was common to leave them wrapped in paper until sold. The table also reveals some unpolished wooden club heads before they were fitted with shafts.

Edward Ray, winner of the Open Championship at Muirfield in 1912. Professional at Oxhey Golf Club near London, he was unfortunate that his career coincided with the glory years of the 'Great Triumvirate' – Vardon, Braid and Taylor. A fine player who was rarely seen without his pipe, his true moment of fame came at the 1920 US Open at Inverness. Becoming one of only three English golfers to have won both the British and American Open titles, he remains a much underrated player.

John Henry Taylor receiving the silver claret jug for winning his fifth Open Championship in 1913 at Royal Liverpool. Only Harry Vardon has ever bettered his record.

John Henry Taylor competing in the Open Championship at Hoylake, 1924. Five-time champion, his career was effectively over by this point, but his famous flat-footed style remained with him throughout his career.

The photograph shows Jock Hutchison, controversial winner of the Open Championship at St Andrews in 1921, in later life. Having beaten the popular English amateur, Roger Wethered in a play-off, St Andrews-born Hutchison returned to his new home in America with howls of criticism ringing in his ears. Having used a new set of deep-grooved irons to hold his approach shots on the sun-baked greens, he was accused of unsportsman-like behaviour. Inevitably the clubs he used were banned in Britain, and despite being twice runner-up in the US Open, his victory at St Andrews was quietly written off as a golfing fluke.

Gene Sarazen in full swing during the 1924 Open Championship at Royal Liverpool. He was the first professional in history to win all four major championships during his career. While he was fast becoming one of the most dominant players in the United States, he would have to wait until 1932 to capture his first Open title.

Walter Hagen receiving a congratulatory kiss from his wife after winning the Open at Hoylake in 1924. Having beaten home favourite Ernie Whitcombe into second, the American could then reflect on how he almost missed out on the event completely after stumbling to a first round qualifying score of 83 a few days before.

Walter Hagen sharpens up his iron play shortly before the Open Championship at Sandwich, watched by fellow American Horton Smith, 1928.

Charles Gibson exhibiting at the 1928 Open Championship at Royal St George's Sandwich. Long before manufacturers of golf equipment realised the benefit of showing off their latest wares at events like the Open, Gibson was promoting his 'Star' brand range of irons. The picture seems to show him having second thoughts about his ground-breaking idea.

Walter Hagen escapes from a bunker on his way to winning the Open at Muirfield in 1929.

American legend Walter Hagen congratulates Henry Cotton after the opening round of the 1929 Open at Muirfield. Hagen went on to win that year, while the young Englishman would have to wait five years for his first victory in the championship.

Golf writer Bernard Darwin (far left) accompanies American stars Johnny Farrell (centre) and Gene Sarazen on a practice round at Muirfield for the 1929 Open Championship. Farrell, who eventually finished second, is perhaps best known for having defeated Bobby Jones in a play-off for the US Open title the previous year at Olympic Fields.

Bobby Jones receives the Open trophy after his victory at Hoylake in 1930.

Henry Cotton making his acceptance speech after winning his third Open title at Muirfield, 1948. Sitting directly behind him, next to his wife 'Toots', is the runner-up that year, Irishman Fred Daly.

Max Faulkner playing the final hole in the 1951 Open Championship at Royal Portrush in Northern Ireland. He was the last Englishman to win the title before Tony Jacklin's emotional victory at Royal Lytham in 1969. It was the only time that the course would be used for the Open Championship.

American legend Ben Hogan playing his first ever shot on British soil in the opening practice round for the 1953 Open at Carnoustie. Looking on are British golf writer Percy Huggins and top US amateur Frank Stranahan. Stranahan would eventually finish the championship in a three-way tie for second with Dai Rees, Peter Thomson and Antonio Cerda.

Bobby Locke holding the silver claret jug after completing his fourth Open victory at St Andrews, 1954.

CHAPTER THREE

LADIES ON THE LINKS

Golf in nineteenth-century Scotland was not considered a suitable pastime for the wives of gentlemen. At a time when physical exertion was considered menial and working class, the idea of a woman raising the club above her head was actually quite shocking for most men. In 1890 Lord Wellwood summed up the feelings of many when he wrote: 'The postures and gestures requisite for a full swing are not particularly graceful when the player is clad in female dress.'

Despite most women golfers being restricted to an occasional putt when no one was looking, the general opinion was that even this was too much. A few years earlier, in the *Cornhill Magazine*, one irate golfer expressed his views on playing a match where his opponent's wife came along to watch: 'The links are not the place for women. They talk incessantly, never stand still, and even if they do, the wind won't allow their dresses to stand still!'

This unsuitability to golf was obviously a long-held view north of the border. As early as 1565 Mary, Queen of Scots, was accused at her trial of playing golf on Seton Links only days after the murder of her husband Lord Darnley. Yet before the end of the 1900s a remarkable revolution had taken place in the women's game. The pace of change was slow at first, but within a few years of Lord Wellwood's acerbic comments female golfers could be seen playing golf on almost every course in Scotland.

Quite how this velvet revolution took place is open to question, but certainly the first shot was fired at St Andrews in 1867. The first female-only golf club having been established on land adjacent to the Old Course at St Andrews, a subtle change in attitude began to take place among the gentleman golfers who passed each day. While the course was still little more than an extended putting green, many could not help but be impressed by the skill exhibited in the competitions held there each month. In his book *The Royal and Ancient Game*, published in 1875, Robert Clark wrote: 'The skills of the fair competitors is by no means to be despised. On their own ground, the best of them would be backed freely against the cracks of the R&A.'

While there was still no question of women being allowed to play with their husbands on the Old Course, the growing respect for ladies' golf was indicative of things to come. Within a few years other clubs had been formed in Scotland and England. By 1893 there were enough to form the Ladies Golf Union, bringing with it a framework by which women's championships could be formally sanctioned. The progress from golfing outcasts to respected female golfers had been little short of meteoric. And all this while dressed in a tweed ankle-length skirt, hacking jacket and stiff-collared blouse.

The first British Ladies Championship, held at Royal Lytham in 1893, was also a major turning point for the women's game. It was won by Lady Margaret Scott, who captured the public's imagination with her youthful vigour and free-flowing swing. The daughter of Lord Eldon, she came to personify the game for many people. She was playing at a time when most sporting occasions were considered purely in terms of being fashionable or not, and her victory – and the two that followed – made golf instantly popular among the upper classes. Attractive and personable, she became something of a celebrity in London society, with *Golf Illustrated* describing her game as 'graceful, yet powerful'.

After the departure of Lady Margaret Scott in the late 1890s, the women's game looked for a new golfing heroine. A young girl from Silloth called Cecilia Leitch fitted the bill when she took centre stage in 1910. She went head-to-head against former Open Champion Harold Hilton in a 72-hole challenge match at Sunningdale. Promoted as a real battle of the sexes, the game was watched by hundreds of excited spectators curious to see if this rising young star could topple the famous champion. Playing off the same tees, Leith was compensated for her lack of distance by receiving one stroke every second hole. For Hilton it was never quite enough advantage, as he lost by 2&1.

Not surprisingly, the result of the match received a great deal of publicity. Played at a time when women's issues were at the forefront of the political agenda, her victory was claimed as a triumph for the fledgling women's movement. Men retaliated by saying that Hilton was unfairly handicapped but, with golf increasingly seen as a bastion of male privilege, suffragettes led by Emily Pankhurst responded by pouring acid on greens all over the Home Counties.

Questions were asked in the Houses of Parliament, especially after Liberal Prime Minister David Lloyd George was debagged while playing at Walton Heath. The crisis was reaching boiling point. Members of golf clubs in the Surrey area were asked to put pressure on their wives and daughters to desist from such reckless action. Then in February 1913 the *Suffragette* magazine commented: 'Some people say the suffragettes have acted very unwisely in destroying golf greens because this has made golfers very angry. Yet what is there to fear from their anger? What have [male] golfers ever done for our cause, and what will they ever do, if they are left in peace and quiet to play their game?'

Eventually matters calmed down as women were granted the vote not long afterwards. Yet prejudice remained, and it would be many years before the more exclusive Surrey clubs opened their doors to female golfers. But while golf in Britain kept an uneasy truce, women's golf in the United States was growing fast. Free from the shackles of social convention, the early 1900s saw the emergence of top class players, like sisters Margaret and Harriot Curtis. Dominating the early years of the US Ladies Championship, they would later become famous as the driving force behind the Curtis Cup matches between Britain and America in the '30s.

Another star to emerge from the United States was Glenna Collett. She won her first Ladies Championship in 1922 at Greenbrier, West Virginia, while still a teenager. Considered almost unbeatable, she was described as the 'female Bobby Jones' as she collected another five titles in the next twelve years. Yet perhaps her most famour hour came in 1929 at the British Ladies Championship at St Andrews. Looking for a new challenge, she arrived in Britain blissfully unaware that the greatest woman golfer in the history of the game was coming out of retirement to meet her – the legendary Joyce Wethered.

Before her decision to leave golf behind in 1926, Wethered had been described by Bobby Jones as 'the finest golfer I have ever seen'. She was still only 25, but stories detailing her skill and powers of concentration had become a part of golfing folklore; yet Joyce had found precious little comfort in being a celebrated golfer. A shy, gangling individual, she rarely took part in the social life which surrounded women's golf in the 1920s, preferring instead to practise alone and leave quickly after the presentation ceremony.

Yet despite this seemingly cold attitude, Wethered was universally well liked by her fellow competitors, and by the large galleries which flocked to see her play. Four-time British Ladies Champion, Joyce had found the strain of competing at such a high level increasingly tiresome. Having made the decision to retire shortly after winning her fourth English Ladies title in 1925 at Troon, she spent the next few years catching up on the life she had missed out on.

Taking up salmon fishing, she took little interest in golf and by the time she returned in 1929 she only had a passing knowledge of rising young British golfers like Enid Wilson and Dianne Fishwick. But Collett was different, and when the opportunity arrived to match her skills against the American over her beloved Old Course, the temptation proved too strong. Once there, any doubts that Wethered had lost her competitive edge were quickly dismissed. Reaching the final, she would have been disappointed if she had faced anyone other than Glenna Collett.

Eagerly anticipated, the 36-hole final was watched by over 5,000 people, swarming all over the course to get a better view of the action. It proved a particularly tense affair for both players. Wethered, finding herself five down after just nine holes, fought back well to level the match with a handful of holes remaining. Eventually running out the winner by the narrow margin of 3&1, Joyce reflected on what a 'trying experience' the final had been.

Perhaps feeling she had nothing left to prove, Wethered retired for a second time, still aged just 29. Later persuaded to make an appearance in the first Curtis Cup match at Wentworth in 1932, she refused to play in either the English or British Ladies Championships and this time kept her promise. Yet curiously fate would play an unusual hand two years later.

While working in the golf department at Fortnum and Mason's in London, she had her amateur status revoked by the Ladies Golf Union for giving lessons. Understandably upset, she then received a $30,000 offer from American millionaire Alex Finlay to play a series of exhibitions in the United States. This was a huge amount of money at the time and Joyce reluctantly accepted, sailing off to New York. American golfers welcomed her with open arms. Touring from coast to coast, her matches against Bobby Jones, Gene Sarazen and, not surprisingly, Glenna Collett were always well attended.

Joyce was also matched against the rising new star of US women's golf, former Olympic hurdler 'Babe' Zaharius, playing her twice and winning twice. Once back in England Joyce continued to play in the occasional exhibition match, but sadly it was not until 1947 that she was re-instated as an amateur. Her career over, she retired to Devon as the wife of her former golfing partner Sir John Heathcoat Amory. The greatest woman golfer in history would never hit a golf shot in competitive anger again.

In 1975 she was inducted into the Golf Hall of Fame at Pinehurst, North Carolina, joining latter-day legends like Joanne Carner, Betsy King and Nancy Lopez. Joyce Wethered's place in golfing legend is assured forever.

A keenly fought competition played over the Ladies Putting Course at St Andrews, *c.* 1884. Another feature of playing golf on 'The Himalayas' were the young caddies who frequented the green. While they were only required to carry a single club, the women employed their services in retrieving the ball from the hole – mainly because the fashionable corsets they wore would not allow them to bend down themselves!

Lady Margaret Scott (centre with dark bonnet) poses with the other semi-finalists in the British Ladies Championship at Royal Portrush, 1895. She eventually defeated Miss E. Lythgoe (second from left) by 5&4 in the eighteen-hole final. This helped establish the event as one of national importance.

Lady Margaret Scott, champion lady golfer in 1893, 1894, 1895. The only daughter of the Earl of Eldon, she was able to fine-tune her game on a private course laid out on the family estate at Stowell Park in Gloucester! Blessed with a long flowing swing which propelled the ball far further than many of her contemporaries', her three victories brought some much-needed popularity to the women's game.

Issette Pearson, a central figure in the development of women's golf in the late 1890s. A strenuous campaigner in the cause of women's golf throughout her life, she was instrumental in the formation of the first official Ladies Golf Union in 1893. She also helped organise the first British Ladies Championship, held at St Anne's Golf Club the same year.

Flowing dresses and bonnets as the women take on the men at Newquay in 1903.

Lottie Dodd: six-time singles champion at Wimbledon, she also won the British Ladies Golf Championship at Troon in 1904. There her final against May Hezlet was played in front of a record crowd of 3,000 people! Interestingly, four years later she announced her retirement from competitive golf and took up archery, where she subsequently represented Great Britain in the 1908 Olympic Games! When she finally died in 1960, it is said that she slipped away while listening to the coverage of Wimbledon on the radio.

Dorothy Campbell driving from the first tee at St Andrews in the British Ladies Championship, 1908. While she lost to Maud Titterton that year, Miss Campbell returned the following season to record her first victory in the event.

Miss Gladys Ravenscroft lines up for the cameras before the final of the British Ladies Championship at Turnberry, 1912.

A rather 'vitriolic' cartoon published in March 1913 in *Golf Monthly* shows the damage caused to golf by the Suffragette Movement. With the game considered a bastion of male prejudice, the normal method employed by these women was to dig up the greens using a trowel or pour Vitriol weedkiller on them. The matter was discussed in the Houses of Parliament, and the medal in the top left-hand corner lists those Home County courses already attacked.

An Edwardian actress in golfing pose.

'The Golf Girl'.

With women's golf seen as increasingly fashionable in the early '20s, publicity photographs like this, taken at Stanmore Golf Club near London, were not uncommon for aspiring actresses. Quite how she expected to play in those high heels is anyone's guess!

Joyce Wethered, four-time British Ladies
Champion and five-time English Ladies
Champion. Famously described by Bobby
Jones as 'The finest golfer I have ever seen',
this tall, gangling English woman dominated
female golf in the 1920s. Known for her great
concentration, in one memorable match she
was playing at Sheringham when a steam train
went rattling by only yards from the green.
Without a flicker she holed out her putt and
appeared surprised when someone asked if the
train had put her off. 'What train?' she
replied!

Britain versus America!
Joyce Wethered (left) and
Glenna Collett pose for
the cameras shortly
before their British Ladies
final at St Andrews, 1929.

American Glenna Collett showing some style as she escapes from a bunker during an unofficial GB *versus* USA match at Sunningdale in 1930.

Enid Wilson is shown putting on the twelfth at Sunningdale during an unofficial match between teams of leading British and American women golfers in 1930, played two years before the inaugural Curtis Cup at Wentworth.

The first British Ladies team to face the United States in the Curtis Cup on home soil. Managed by Alex Balfour (left), the match was played at Chevy Chase Country Club in 1934. Having already lost the opening encounter two years earlier at Wentworth, they would lose again, this time by the margin of 6½ to 2½.

In 1890 Lord Wellwood spoke on behalf of many men when he wrote: 'The postures and gestures requisite for a full swing are not particularly graceful when the player is clad in female dress.' Quite what he would have thought about the 'female dress' of this young actress from 1950 is not known.

The legendary American professional 'Babe' Didrikson Zaharius. A remarkable athlete, she was an All-American basketball player, track star in the 1932 Olympics and accomplished swimmer, dancer and tennis player. Turning to competitive golf in 1945, she immediately became a prolific tournament winner and instant celebrity with her booming 250 yard drives. In 1954 she capped off a wonderful career by winning her third US Open title by a massive twelve strokes.

CHAPTER FOUR

BOBBY JONES & THE STORY OF EARLY AMERICAN GOLF

Where and when golf was first played in the United States is open to question. While the first golf club was formed in New York in 1888, it was thought that the game had been played at least one hundred years before. Reports in a Charleston newspaper actually mention the formation of the Harleston Green Golf Club in 1786. At the same time, across the state border in Savannah, another early golf course was also described in a newspaper report of the time. Quite how these early links came about is not explained, and neither has what eventually happened to them.

What is certain is that after the aptly named St Andrews Golf Club was established in the late nineteenth century, golf in America took off at an alarming rate. From those first primitive beginnings in a Yonkers cow pasture, using golf clubs bought from 'Old' Tom Morris himself, the club and its enthusiastic membership moved to a new 34 acre site in North Broadway, the site of an old orchard. It was only a matter of time before the group of golfing friends were labelled the 'Apple Tree Gang'.

As their numbers grew, so inevitably did the need for a larger area to play on. Having established the game's popularity in the New York area, the club moved at least once more before finally relocating to their present home at Mount Hope in 1897. But by that time golf had changed beyond all recognition from the amateurish pastime it had been fewer than ten years earlier.

With golf clubs being formed almost every few months, the growing popularity of the sport was attracting interest from big money investors. In 1891 Shinnecock Hills was built on nearby Long Island – a long-time holiday resort of the rich and famous. Designed by Scottish course architect Willie Dunn, it involved twelve holes built along the Great Peconic Bay, and is still considered among the most scenic of all early American courses.

In keeping with this luxurious style, the Brookline Country Club just outside Boston was built in 1892. Yet perhaps the most prestigious of all these early golf clubs was the nine-hole course at Newport, Rhode Island. The club was formed in 1890 by a syndicate of millionaires including Cornelius Vanderbilt, Theodore Havermayer and America's richest man, John Jacob Astor, and was selected as the venue for the inaugural United States Open Championship in 1895.

The idea of having a national championship had been suggested the year before at a meeting of the newly formed Amateur Golf Association of the United States (later to become the United States Golf Association), attended by representatives of all the main clubs, plus the first golf club in the mid-west, Chicago. Theodore Havermayer was elected the first president over John Reid – the person credited with forming the St Andrews Golf Club. It was also agreed that two competitions would be held the following year – one for professionals and the other for amateurs – and held during the same week.

The amateur event took precedence, and the first winner was Charles Blair MacDonald. A highly belligerent man, he had dismissed the result of an earlier championship in which he had come second because he did not like the result! Later becoming one of the most influential members of the USGA, it was his constant blustering about the rules which had led to the forming of a national committee in the first place. Given the task of organising both the Open and Amateur Championships, he later proved a tireless worker despite his former attitude to authority.

There were few home-grown professionals, so the early years of what became the United States Open was dominated by ex-patriot Scots, Fred Herd, James Foulis and the Smith brothers, Alex and Willie. In 1900 the competition was given a real boost when the legendary Harry Vardon came over to compete during a tour sponsored by the Spalding Golf Company. Winning with ease, he returned in 1913 convinced that it would be the same story over again, but what followed has since gone down in US Open folklore.

Francis Ouimet was a former caddie whose world could not have been further removed from the rich lifestyle enjoyed by those for whom he worked. Although still an amateur, he entered the US Open at Brookline mainly because it was the course he knew best. Having already used up his vacation time at Wright and Ditson, where he was employed in the sporting goods department, he begged to be let off to compete. Once there, he found himself tied after three rounds with both Vardon and another British star, Ted Ray. With the final round played that afternoon and the course playing long after heavy overnight rain, the 20 year old went out determined not to fall away as many had expected.

Having troubles of his own, Ouimet struggled out in 43 and looked to have blown his chances of winning. Yet after over-hearing comments made in the crowd about him not being good enough, he settled down with two birdies over the closing holes to finish still tied with Vardon and Ray. Returning the following day, when the excitement caused by his appearance in the eighteen-hole play-off could not have been greater, he remained remarkably calm despite all the noise that followed the match – no doubt calmed by his 10-year-old caddy Eddie Lowery, who kept whispering 'be sure and keep your eye on the ball'. Ouimet took his advice and played the round of his life.

Finally going ahead on the tenth, Ouimet's steady play put so much pressure on Harry Vardon that he lit up a cigarette – something he never did during a tournament. In the end, Ouimet's round of 72 was enough to see off both British professionals, with Vardon scoring 77 to Ray's 78. In the eyes of many the young man had done the impossible. Not only that, he inspired countless thousands of young Americans to take up the game for themselves.

Today it is difficult to assess just how much Francis Ouimet's victory in the US Open at Brookline contributed to the amazing growth in golf over the coming years. Famed golf writer

Herbert Warren Wind wrote later: 'Had a pleasant young man from a good Fifth Avenue family or some stiff and staid professional beaten Vardon and Ray, it is really doubtful whether his victory would have been the wholesale therapeutic for American golf that it was'. What is certain is that when another charismatic young amateur, called Bobby Jones, came along twenty years later, the effect on the American game was just as electrifying.

It has been said that if Francis Ouimet lit the flame of golf interest in America, then Bobby Jones started the bonfire. Indeed, no golfer in the history of the game has ever come closer to achieving mythical status than Robert Tyre Jones junior did in the late 1920s. A golfing genius, he was also a successful businessman, author, club designer and qualified lawyer. And if that was not enough, he also became the founder of Augusta National Golf Club in Georgia – the home of the US Masters.

Remaining an amateur throughout his career, he competed against and consistently beat some of the greatest professionals the game has ever known – blessed with a smooth rhythmic swing, sure-fire putting stroke and flawless temperament. His record was nothing less than remarkable: between 1923 and 1930 he won a total of thirteen major titles including five US Amateurs, four US Opens, three British Opens and one British Amateur.

But the achievement Jones is best remembered for is his 'Grand Slam' of 1930. Never emulated before or since, his clean sweep of all four major titles in one year, amateur and professional, made him a legend in his own lifetime. With no more worlds to conquer, he then retired from competitive golf later the same year, aged 28. Since then Bobby Jones has become the yardstick against which all other great golfers are measured.

Born in Atlanta on 17 March 1902, Jones was considered a golfing prodigy by the time he was 12. Growing up close to the East Lake Golf Club, where his parents rented rooms in a nearby boarding house, the game had been a constant in his life since early childhood. A digestive illness left him frail and unable to eat solid foods until well after his sixth birthday, yet he grew up physically strong and was able to power the ball surprisingly long distances.

In 1916 he entered his first US Amateur Championship at Merion Cricket Club in Philadelphia. Having to play a pre-qualifying round before the matchplay stages, Jones' excellent score of 74 created a minor sensation. Still only 14, his reputation was further enhanced when he made it through two rounds before being beaten by a former champion. Making swift progress over the next few years, his biggest success after that was finishing tied second behind Gene Sarazen in the US Open at Chicago in 1922.

Graduating from Georgia Tech the same year, Bobby Jones enrolled at Harvard seeking his MA degree. While golf was his first love, it seemed that he had no intention of turning professional – now or in the future. Later qualifying as a lawyer, he had always known that golf would never be considered a suitable occupation for a southern gentleman. Yet for now competition was in his blood, and despite being acknowledged as one of the finest amateurs in the country Jones had not actually won anything.

Aged 20, he resolved to change this record with the US Open at Inwood Country Club the following year. Jones played well enough on the tight, tree-lined golf course to tie championship leader Bobby Cruickshank after four rounds. In the exciting eighteen-hole play-off both men played to the top of their form, with only three holes halved all day. First Jones had taken the lead, then Cruickshank. Coming down the final hole, the result was still in the balance until the young Atlanta golfer ripped his approach shot 200 yards through the air to within a few feet of the hole. If ever one shot influenced golf history then it was this one. Tapping in for the first major victory of his career, Bobby Jones had finally arrived in the big-time.

If the first seven years of Bobby Jones career can be described as famine, the next seven were certainly feast. By the time he came to Britain for the Walker Cup in 1926 he had won two national Amateur titles and had been twice runner-up in the US Open. He also wanted to dispel the memory of his last trip to Scotland, when not only had he performed badly but had disgraced himself at the 'Home of Golf' by storming off the Old Course during the Open in 1921. Back then the pressure had got to him and, despite his enviable record, there were still those who doubted his ability to win under real pressure.

Determined to prove himself a changed man, Bobby Jones was in examplary form both on and off the course. Playing some of the best golf of his life, he helped the United States to a 6–5 victory over Great Britain, and beat off Al Watrous to win his first Open Championship at Royal Lytham. Returning to New York with his team, Jones was awarded a ticker tape parade down Fifth Avenue and congratulated by the Mayor on the steps of the City Hall. For the first time in the history of the United States, golf had made the front page of the national newspapers.

Then almost before the paper had been swept away, Bobby Jones was again in action at the US Open at Scioto Country Club in Columbus, Ohio. Huge crowds turned out to watch him make it an Open double. He did not disappoint them, beating Joe Turnesa into second place. It heralded the most successful period of his golfing life, including his legendary 'Grand Slam'.

Over the next few years Jones steadily added to his collection of championship titles, including the 1929 US Open at Winged Foot. Having now established his own busy law practice in Atlanta, he knew that his career was coming to an end. The strain of tournament play, the long days spent travelling and the lack of any real family life was beginning to tell. As he approached the new decade, Jones knew that 1930 could possibly be his final year in competitive golf. But as the history books show, it would also be his greatest.

Arriving in Britain as the newly elected captain of the American Walker Cup side, Jones set about winning the British Amateur at St Andrews. Meeting his old rival Roger Wethered in the thirty-six hole final, Jones demolished the popular English player by a score of 7&5. Despite this, crowds of enthusiastic well-wishers mobbed the American, who only managed to get back to the clubhouse with the help of a police escort.

The same scenes greeted him at Hoylake for the second leg of his 'Grand Slam'. Competing in the Open Championship, he stumbled to closing rounds of 74–75, and was forced to wait as Leo Deigel and MacDonald Smith made a strong closing challenge. Ultimately it was never going to be enough, and Bobby Jones returned to the United States with the British 'double' under his belt.

After Royal Liverpool came Interlachen in Minneapolis at the US Open Championship. On the opening day record crowds in excess of 10,000 roamed the sunbaked fairways trying to get any view of the action. Under intense pressure from Tommy Armour and the in-form

MacDonald Smith, Jones holed an incredible 50 foot putt on the final green to win his fourth National Open title.

A few weeks later in the US Amateur at Merion, the scene of his major championship debut all those years earlier, Bobby Jones finally made it four in a row. Playing in front of 18,000 people, he beat the hapless Eugene Homans by 8&7 in the final and completed an unprecedented full house of all major titles. In the weeks that followed he took some time away with his wife Mary and considered his options. When he finally did return it was to shock the golfing world with the announcement that he was giving up tournament golf forever. He was aged just 28.

Content to stay out of the tournament spotlight, Bobby Jones concentrated his efforts on a wider range of golfing projects. Not least among these was building his dream golf course back in his home state of Georgia. In December 1930 dreams started to become reality when he was invited by New York banker Clifford Roberts to view an old fruit plantation near the small town of Augusta. Excited by the possibility of constructing a golf course among the magnolia and dogwood, Bobby Jones took little persuading that this was indeed the spot.

With property prices hit hard by the depression, Jones assembled a group of wealthy investors to buy the land and help with the formation of a private members club. Employing

This photograph is commonly referred to as the first photograph of early American golf. Showing the St Andrews Golf Club in Yonkers in 1888, it reveals the old cow pasture where the game was first played by the golfing pioneers. Left to right: Harry Holbrook, A.P. Kinnan, J.B. Upham and John Reid.

renowned Scottish course architect Alister MacKenzie to help design the course, Jones set about building eighteen individual holes that would not only prove challenging but fair.

With work beginning in spring 1931, the newly named Augusta National Golf Club was finished by autumn 1932. Designed with wide-open fairways, large undulating greens and only twenty-two bunkers, the course itself was considered somewhat revolutionary. Yet no one could deny how well it fitted in with the natural surroundings, and when asked what he thought MacKenzie described it simply as 'my finest achievement'.

While Bobby Jones had used ideas gleaned from his tournament career in the design of each hole, it was never his intention that Augusta National should be anything more than a private members course. Yet with the course's reputation spreading far beyond the southern heartland, it was not long before the USGA approached Jones about staging a professional event there – possibly even the National Open.

At first the idea was rejected, but soon the pressure began to build on Augusta National to hold at least some sort of tournament. After some debate it was decided that Bobby Jones should 'invite' some of his golfing chums along for a private competition. The fact that this event included a prize fund of $5,000 and a list of top professionals was quietly ignored.

The tournament was scheduled for the last weekend in March 1934; Jones himself was a reluctant participant in the whole affair. Eventually relenting, he was persuaded by Clifford Roberts that 'it would be wrong to invite people along and not turn up yourself'. However, Jones did get his way over the title of the competition. Roberts had wanted to call it the Masters, while Jones still preferred the less pompous Augusta National Invitational.

Inevitably news of a Bobby Jones comeback filled the sporting headlines for weeks. Still only 32, Jones had played well in practice, even shooting a course record 65. But he knew better than anyone that practice and tournament play were totally different, and so it proved. Struggling desperately to find his putting touch on the fast greens, he rattled off rounds of 76–74–72–72 to finish ten shots behind the eventual winner, Horton Smith. Despite this, the tournament was deemed a resounding success by players and press alike.

The following year at Augusta the newly titled Masters was home to one of the most spectacular shots in the history of golf. Chasing the clubhouse leader Craig Wood, the diminutive Gene Sarazen holed out his second shot on the long par 5, fifteen in the final round on his way to winning. Later described as 'the shot heard all round the world', it enforced the competition's growing reputation for dramatic action and close finishes.

Today the roll call of Masters winners reads like a 'Who's Who' of golfing greats. While neither Bobby Jones, Francis Ouimet or, indeed, C.B. MacDonald are on that list, their place in American golfing history is well assured.

Golfers and caddies at Charleston, South Carolina, *c.* 1900. The social divisions were evident even on the links.

Mowing the greens the hard way: golf course maintenance at Shinnecock Hills, *c.* 1900.

A rare group photograph taken during the 1897 US Open at Chicago; among those pictured are some of the most important names in US golf. Standing, left to right: Alex Smith, Robert Foulis, David Foulis and Alex Findlay. Seated: Fred Herd, James Foulis and Horace Rawlins. Smith and Rawlins, along with Willie Dunn junior (runner-up in the first US Open at Newport in 1895) and Willie Anderson (Smith's great arch rival), between them either won or finished second in ten out of the first twelve US Opens from 1895 onward.

This early photograph of US golf, taken in Denver, Colorado, in 1898, shows how the opening drive had to be hit over the local horse racing track.

Left: Fred Herd, winner of the 1898 US Open Championship at Myopia. Right: Fred Herd, pictured with his younger brother, David. While Fred took on American citizenship and was rarely seen without his winners medal (left), David failed to settle in the New World and later returned as club professional to Littlestone in Sussex.

Harry Vardon during his first exhibition tour of the United States in 1900, paid for by Spalding Sporting Goods Co. The primary idea was to promote the new 'Vardon Flyer' golf ball.

Walter Travis, the first American winner of the British Amateur Championship, 1904. Known somewhat unkindly as the 'Old Man' of US golf, he also won the US Amateur title three times and was once runner-up in the US Open. He was known for his excellent use of the aluminium-headed Schenectady putter (pictured), which was later outlawed in Britain as it made the game 'far too easy'!

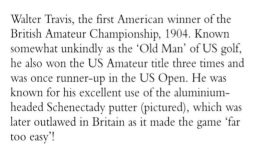

Francis Ouimet posing for the camera shortly after his remarkable victory in the 1913 US Open at the Country Club, Brookline. Having defeated British stars, Harry Vardon and Ted Ray in the eighteen-hole play-off, the former caddy became an instant celebrity.

American Francis Ouimet pictured between British professionals Harry Vardon (left) and Ted Ray shortly before the play-off for the 1914 Open at Brookline.

John D. Rockefeller, aged 80, reputed to be the richest man in the world when this photograph was taken in 1919. A keen golfer, he employed noted golf course architect Donald Ross to design another nine holes for his private golf course at Overhills, North Carolina – a course only he and his closest friends ever got to play.

From left to right, Alex Herd, Gene Sarazen and J.H. Taylor pose for the camera at the 1920 US Open at Inverness.

This informal photograph shows the United States amateur team which played Great Britain in 1921. It is important for two reasons. The match itself was held at Royal Liverpool and proved to be the forerunner of the Walker Cup and Ryder Cup matches between the two. With America ultimately victorious by 9–3, it was also the first overseas tournament appearance of Bobby Jones (second from right). Also shown are, from left to right, William Fownes, Wood Platt, Fred Wright, Francis Ouimet, Paul Hunter and Jesse Guilford.

Gene Sarazen, the first professional in history to win all four major championships during his career. Here he is pictured after winning his first US Open title at Skokie in 1922, swinging a hickory shafted driver. His winners medal can be seen suspended from his waistband.

'Playing Hoop Golf in 1922'. Professionals at White Sulpher Springs Resort, West Virginia, Sammy Belfore (left) and Art Susa show what fun it can be hitting a ball through a fire alarm ring!

American professional Bobby Cruickshank. While he never represented the USA in the Ryder Cup, he was perhaps best known for losing to Bobby Jones in a play-off for the US Open at Inwood Country Club in 1923.

Golf comes to Broadway in the early '20s! In England at the time it was still frowned upon if a woman golfer showed her ankles while out on the links.

In the United States of the mid-'20s golf increasingly became a game for the successful company executive. This photograph shows a typical lunchtime chip and putt competition on top of a New York skyscraper.

Tommy Armour, nicknamed the 'Silver Scot', is shown putting on the final green in the play-off for the 1927 United States Open at Oakmont. Having tied with Harry 'Lighthorse' Cooper after four rounds, the ex-patriot Scot then went on to defeat his American opponent by three strokes – 76 to 79.

Still in his US Airforce uniform, Horton Smith poses for the camera with British star Henry Cotton at Wentworth in 1945.

The legendary hard hitting, hard living Scottish professional Tommy Armour, shown here receiving the US Open trophy in 1927.

The 1928 US Walker Cup side face Great Britain at Chicago with Bobby Jones sitting centre and Francis Ouimet sitting far left. Not surprisingly, the result was a 13–1 thrashing for the visitors.

The unusual putting style of American professional Leo Deigel, shown here during the 1929 Open Championship at Muirfield. Plagued by putting problems throughout his career, he later swapped this elbows-in, crouching style for a one-handed method and a 12 inch long putter!

An early photograph of golf at Pine Valley, late 1920s.

Two legends of American golf greet each other shortly before the 1929 US Open at Winged Foot – Bobby Jones and Walter Hagen.

The immortal Robert Tyre Jones junior – perhaps the greatest golfer who ever lived, photographed here in 1930, his 'Grand Slam' year.

Bobby Jones competing in the *Golf Illustrated* Gold Vase tournament at Sunningdale in 1930. Later the same year the American would complete his legendary 'Grand Slam' of British and American, Open and Amateur Championships. Having achieved the impossible, the American amateur then amazed the world by announcing his retirement at the age of 28. Yet golf did not lose him completely. In the next few years he helped design and build Augusta National Golf Club in Georgia – the home of the prestigious US Masters event. Today he is considered one of the greatest golfers ever to have played the game.

Bobby Jones playing one of the most famous shots in golf history. Competing in the 1930 British Amateur at St Andrews, he played ex-coal miner Sid Roper in the opening round. In what proved the first step in his legendary 'Grand Slam' year, Jones drove his ball into Cottage bunker to the right of the fourth fairway. Hard against the back face, and still over 140 yards from the hole, he managed to hole his approach. Eventually winning on the sixteenth, his eagle-two was perhaps the most spectacular shot of the tournament.

Bobby Jones practising hard with his putter 'Calamity Jane' during the 1930 Amateur Championship at St Andrews in 1930.

Bobby Jones in full swing against Englishman Roger Wethered in the final of the British Amateur at St Andrews, 1930. With the American eventually winning by 7&6, it would later prove the first leg in what became his 'Grand Slam' season.

'Three down, with just one to go.' A thoughtful Bobby Jones receives the 1930 United States Open trophy from USGA President Findley Douglas after beating a top class field at Interlachen. Having already won the British Amateur at St Andrews and the Open at Royal Liverpool earlier in the year, Jones was now well on his way to achieving his legendary 'Grand Slam', something he would achieve a few weeks later at Merion by capturing the US Amateur title.

Bobby Jones poses with the British Open trophy, the US Open and Amateur trophies and the Walker Cup, late 1930. Interestingly, the large cup awarded for the British Amateur Championship is missing from his 'Grand Slam' collection.

President Dwight D. Eisenhower enjoying a game at Turnberry in 1959. Along with Arnold Palmer, his love of golf helped boost the sport's popularity in the United States in the early '60s.

The stylish Horton Smith competing in the USA versus Northern Professionals match at Royal Aberdeen, 1930. Partnering his fellow American Leo Deigel (behind with hat), he will always be remembered as the first winner of the US Masters at Augusta in 1934.

'The most unusual golf course in the world.' Arizona is now one of the most popular tourist destinations for golfers world wide, but back in 1930 it was a big talking point, having a golf course in the middle of a desert. The photographer describes the image, taken at Squaw Peak near Phoenix, as 'simply spectacular'.

American professional Jack Fleck putting on the final green at Olympic Golf Club in San Francisco in the 1955 United States Open. A complete unknown, he safely two-putted for par to tie Ben Hogan on a four round total of 287. The following day he pulled off one of the greatest of all Open upsets by defeating the previously invincible Hogan by three shots in the play-off – 69 to 72.

The legendary American professional Ben Hogan.

A rare photograph of the great Jack Nicklaus taken while he was still an amateur in the early 1960s.

CHAPTER FIVE

THE RYDER CUP

From humble beginnings the Ryder Cup has evolved into one of the great sporting occasions of the modern era. Played since the days of hickory shafted clubs, these dramatic head-to-head encounters between the best golfers of Europe and the United States have captured the imagination of sports lovers worldwide. The *New York Times* once described the hotly contested biannual matches as 'golf at its ultimate best'.

Yet long before Sam Ryder entered the picture, legendary American golfer Walter Hagen had already suggested bringing over a US team to Britain to play 'the locals' at Gleneagles. Old-time Scottish champion Andrew Kirkaldy is reported to have dismissed the idea, scheduled for June 1921, declaring 'It will be too one-sided – the Americans haven't got a prayer.' And so it proved. Even with Scottish exiles like Tommy Armour and Jock Hutchison playing for their newly adopted country, they were soundly beaten by 9–3.

Hagen tried again in 1926. With pre-qualifying for the Open Championship held at Sunningdale, he was invited by wealthy St Albans seed merchant Samuel Ryder to captain an American team to take on the British at nearby Wentworth. The result this time was an even more embarrassing defeat by 13½–1½, with Hagen put to the sword by George Duncan 6&5 in the singles.

Yet despite the margin of defeat Hagen responded positively to a further suggestion by Sam Ryder that the matches should be continued on a more formal 'home and away' basis. Ryder himself had watched some of the action and was impressed by the spirit of camaraderie between the two sets of professionals. Prompted by Duncan, he agreed to provide a suitable trophy for the two teams to play for, later commissioning Mappin and Webb to make one at the cost of £25. The Ryder Cup was finally underway.

Even before the first official match got underway on 3 and 4 June 1927, at Worcester Country Club, Massachusetts, Sam Ryder had long since made his mark as a benevolent sponsor of professional golfing events. Four years earlier, in 1923, he had invited players of the quality of Harry Vardon and J.H. Taylor to compete in a tournament at his home club of Verulam in Hertfordshire.

Named after his Heath and Heather Seed Company, each professional received an appearance fee of £5 with the eventual winner, Arthur Havers, receiving £50. Considered somewhat controversial at the time, it was only £25 less than he got for winning the Open that year!

Among the other professionals competing in the event was Abe Mitchell. Described as the best golfer never to win the Open, he was a highly respected figure in the British game in the 1920s. A close friend of Sam Ryder, he was retained as his personal golf tutor at the princely sum of £1,000 per annum. With the two men sharing an abiding passion for all things golfing, it came as no surprise when Ryder asked for his image to adorn the lid of the new golden trophy.

After the victory at Wentworth in 1926, it was considered a foregone conclusion that Britain would come home victorious from the inaugural Ryder Cup in the United States. Yet even before the match got underway disaster struck the 'home' team. Shortly before the British team was due to set sail on the liner *Aquitania*, Mitchell, elected team captain only a few weeks earlier, fell ill with appendicitis. It was a cruel blow for everyone concerned as the talented Englishman was forced to stay at home. Commiserating with his loss, Ryder later wrote to him, saying: 'Let us hope our team can win, but it is the play without the Prince of Denmark.'

In New York harbour, all custom formalities being waived, the British side were greeted by brass bands and a welcome speech from the city mayor. Accompanied by a motor-cycle escort, they were then whisked away in a fleet of chauffeur-driven limousines through downtown Manhattan to their luxury hotel. In the days that followed banquets and champagne receptions were arranged in their honour, with the cream of New York society turning out to meet them. Coming from the austere, depressed Britain of the 1920s, many of the working-class professionals were completely overwhelmed by this extravagant display of American hospitality.

Almost inevitably the British team, now captained by former Open Champion Ted Ray, suffered a heavy defeat at the hands of the United States by 9½–2½. Back home, the result was a real shock. Having launched a £3,000 appeal to send the team over to America, the editor of *Golf Illustrated*, George Philpot, wrote in his magazine that Britain should have awarded itself the Cup in 1926 as a kind of tonic. It was a humorous suggestion, yet nothing could lessen the palpable sense of dismay home golfers felt about such a humiliating loss. Indeed, the only consolation was that Sam Ryder was spared the indignity of watching the match because of his fear of long sea crossings.

The second match was played on 27–8 April 1929 at Moortown in Leeds. Once again, the Americans took the early initiative, winning the opening day foursomes 2½–1½. With eight singles remaining, it looked as if it would be yet another USA triumph, but matters were not as clear-cut as they seemed. One infamous tale that has now become part of Ryder Cup folklore concerned the old rivals Walter Hagen and George Duncan.

After finding that he had been drawn to play the 1920 Open champion in the second match, Hagen had boasted to his team: 'Well boys, that's one sure point for us.' Somehow Duncan got wind of his opponent's rash comments and blasted him off the golf course the following day by the astounding margin of 10&8! With Archie Compston beating the highly rated Gene Sarazen and further losses for Watrous, Turnesa and Farrell, it left a shell-shocked American team wondering what they had done to deserve such punishment. With the final result 7–5 to the home side, British pride was restored, leaving the series tied at one each.

Thus the Ryder Cup was under way, played every two years with the venue alternating between Britain and the United States. In December that year Sam Ryder made a gift of his elegant trophy to the fledgling British PGA, rather than presenting it to the R&A. Even though the Scottish Golf Club ran the Open Championship, he felt the professionals themselves were the best people to administer future Ryder Cups, and signed a Deed of Trust to that effect.

From the comparative cold of Yorkshire, the 1931 match now moved on to Scioto Country Club in Columbus, Ohio, in the searing heat of summer. With temperatures permanently in the high nineties, British team manager Fred Pignon described the difficulties his players faced: 'in this weather golf is not a game – it is a form of torture.'

Forced to play without their best player, Henry Cotton, because of a petty squabble over travelling arrangements, little hope was given to the first 'away' victory in the series. Yet Cotton's absence was probably a double-edged sword for the British camp.

Public school educated, Cotton was considered stand-offish by many of his fellow professionals. At best an infrequent supporter of the Ryder Cup, he had already affected team morale in the run up to the match with his demands for a larger percentage of the pooled money won by British players in tournaments before and after the match. On the other hand, Cotton was the best prospect for years and was desperately needed against an increasingly strong American side. Inevitably, the match at Scioto was lost before it had even begun.

The history of the Ryder Cup, especially in recent years, has been littered with close results and heart-stopping final days. Among the best was the match held at Southport and Ainsdale Golf Club in 1933. J.H. Taylor was nominated non-playing captain, and immediately ordered a strict fitness regime for his players which involved early morning workouts on nearby Southport Sands.

Played in front of record crowds, victory in the opening foursomes left the British team needing only a share of the singles to win. Watched by the heir to the English throne, Edward, Prince of Wales, the match balanced on a knife edge all afternoon until it finally came down to the final game between Syd Easterbrook and American Denny Shute.

In scenes reminiscent of later matches at the Belfry, Shute missed from 3 feet on the last leaving the English professional a tap-in for an overall victory by 6½–5½. At the presentation later, the Prince summed up the feelings of everyone when he said: 'In giving this Cup, I am naturally impartial, but of course we over here are very pleased to have won.'

If Southport in 1933 was a high point for Great Britain and Ireland, then the match at Ridgewood, New Jersey, two years later was a depressing low. With Cotton again excluded from the match because of the PGA's provision that all players should be resident in Britain at the time of selection (he was club professional at Royal Waterloo in Belgium), defeat was not totally unexpected. With press criticism ringing in their ears for a catalogue of inept individual performances, the British team ran out losers by 9–3.

The tide had finally changed. In Britain the halcyon days of Vardon, Braid and Taylor were just a memory, with the United States now the dominant force in world golf. The reasons were simple. The ever-expanding American PGA Tour was now producing a conveyer belt of competition-hardened players the quality of Sam Snead and Tony Manero, while top British professionals were forced to hold down club posts just to make a living.

The balance of power had shifted, and even with the decline of Hagen and Sarazen the writing was now well and truly on the wall. In 1937 the United States returned to the scene of their previous defeat, Southport and Ainsdale. Running out winners by 8–4, they inflicted the first 'home' defeat in the Ryder Cup's short history. Sadly for the British team and those home supporters it would not be the last.

Even before the ten year break for the war, the matches were no longer competitive. In 1947 an out of practice British side took on the United States at Portland, Oregon and lost by 11–1. Two years later the Ryder Cup was staged at Ganton in Yorkshire, and once more Britain came off worse 7 matches to 5.

There was better news for Britain at Wentworth in 1953. With the young Peter Alliss making his Ryder Cup debut, the match proved an exciting one for all concerned. Going down to the wire, the home side recovered from a 3–1 defeat in the foursomes to stand on the threshold of a remarkable victory, with only two games remaining in the final day singles. Everything, it turned out, depended on Alliss and another new boy, Bernhard Hunt. Sadly the future golfing pundit faltered on the final hole to give Joe Turnesa an unexpected win, while Hunt did the same in his halved match with Dale Douglas. The result, yet another victory to the United States by the narrow margin of 6½–5½.

While Britain still continued to produce fine individual players like Dai Rees and the 1951 Open champion, Max Faulkner, the Americans always had the strength in depth. Consequently, in the next nineteen matches the United States would only lose one.

At Lindrick Golf Club in 1957, the British side credited their win as much to bloody-minded determination as golfing skill. Typical of this was the no-nonsense Scottish pro Eric Brown. Having been soundly beaten by the equally bad-tempered American Tommy Bolt in the opening day foursomes – a series Britain lost 3–1 – he resolved to get his revenge in the singles the following day. Playing first, he refused to speak all the way round, eventually beating the legendary 'Lightning' Bolt by 4&3. It had been a tough match, and when they shook hands afterward, the American commented on how little he had enjoyed the game – to which Brown replied: 'And nor would I after the licking I've just given you.'

Later some of the Americans complained bitterly about the treatment they had received at the hands of the British crowds. But what could they really expect, as the home side won 6½ out of the 8 points available on that memorable final day. Eventually strolling to a 7½–4½ victory, little did anybody know that it would be the last ever victory in the Ryder Cup for a British side.

After Lindrick, it would be another twelve years before a British side would go close again. Now part of golf history, Jack Nicklaus conceded Tony Jacklin his short putt on the final green of the 1969 match at Royal Birkdale to halve the entire match at 16–16. But as far as the United States were concerned, it was not enough to resurrect the event as a worthwhile competition. After another crushing defeat for Britain at Royal Lytham in 1977, the decision was made to make the Ryder Cup a USA versus Europe affair.

Ultimately it was the right choice. Despite complaints from the traditionalists, the matches have gone on from strength to strength in the modern era. With the two sides now perfectly matched, it has long been one of the most eagerly anticipated events of the golfing calendar, still played to the highest levels of sportsmanship. Old Sam Ryder would be delighted to see how his 'little' match has turned out.

Samuel Ryder, the face behind the trophy.

Before the first Ryder Cup was played in 1927, Sam Ryder (centre) was a keen sponsor of British professional golf in the '20s. Here he is shown shortly before an 'England versus Scotland International Foursome' between (left to right) Harry Vardon and J.H. Taylor and Alex Herd and James Braid, played at Verulam Golf Club, St Albans, in 1926. The English pair eventually ran out winners by 10&8. The finest golfers of their era, none of the four was considered for the first British Ryder Cup side to face the Americans at Worcester, Massachusetts, less than one year later.

Alexander ('Sandy') Herd competing in the 'International Foursomes' match arranged by Sam Ryder at Verulam Golf Club, September 1926.

Walter Hagen and Ted Ray discuss the merits of team golf at Wentworth, 1926. The year before the first official Ryder Cup got underway at Worcester, Massachusetts, an unofficial match was played between teams of British and American professionals. The final result was 13–1 to the home side with one match halved.

Open Champion in 1920, George Duncan. Famous for the quickness of his play, his later autobiography was appropriately titled *Golf at the Gallop*. And while English professional Duncan would never win another Open, he would prove a mainstay in the British team's effort to win the Ryder Cup in the '20s and '30s.

British Ryder Cup player Aubrey Boomer, 1926.

The victorious United States Ryder Cup team at Worcester, 1927. The first match in the long running series, the American side ran out winners over the British by 9–2. From left to right: Al Watrous, Bill Melhorn, Leo Diegel, Johnny Golden, Walter Hagen, Al Espinosa, Gene Sarazen, Johnny Farrell and Joe Turnesa.

'Professionals v. Amateurs' at Coombe Hill, 1929. Organised as a practice match for the forthcoming Ryder Cup at Moortown, it includes (from left to right) British professionals Archie Compston and George Duncan against Roger Wethered and Major Hezlet for the amateurs.

The first United States Ryder Cup team to visit Britain, 1929, photographed on board the *Mauretania*. They would ultimately fail to defend the trophy won two years earlier at Worcester. Standing, left to right: Ed Dudley, Al Watrous, Gene Sarazen, Leo Diegel, Al Espinosa and Johnny Farrell. Kneeling: Horton Smith, Walter Hagen, Joe Turnesa and Johnny Golden.

Walter Hagen, captain of the 1929 USA Ryder Cup team, disembarks from the *Mauretania* at Plymouth before travelling up to Moortown in Leeds for the match. Never one to travel second class, the flamboyant American's famous motto was 'Never hurry, never worry, always stop along the way and smell the flowers.'

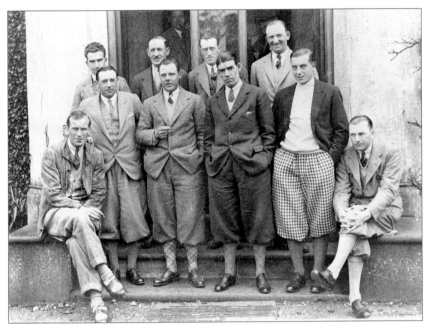

The British Ryder Cup team to face the Americans at Moortown, 1929. The first time the match was played in England, it ended in a rare home victory by 7–5. Back row, left to right: Stewart Burns, Abe Mitchell, Charlie Whitcombe, Fred Robson. Front row: Ernie Whitcombe, Percy Alliss, George Duncan, Henry Cotton. Seated: Archie Compston and Aubrey Boomer.

Aubrey Boomer (left) takes the opportunity to exchange clubs with Americans Johnny Golden (centre) and Al Watrous (right), during practice for the 1929 Ryder Cup at Moortown, Leeds. In Britain, the hickory-shafted clubs of the British side contrasted starkly with the steel-shafted clubs of the USA.

Walter Hagen, captain of the 1929 team,
shows off the Ryder Cup soon after
arriving in Britain. He would return
home without it after his team was
surprisingly defeated at Moortown in
Leeds by the narrow margin of 7–5.

Sam Ryder hands over the trophy to
winning British captain George Duncan at
Moortown, 1929. In the final day singles
Duncan had been drawn to play the US
captain Walter Hagen. On hearing this, the
American reputedly said to his team mates:
'Well boys, there's a certain point for us
right there.' Somehow Duncan got to hear
of this, and went out the following day – to
demolish Hagen by the embarrassing score
of 10&8!

Sam Ryder bids farewell to Abe Mitchell at Waterloo prior to the Ryder Cup match at Scioto in 1931. Old friend Mitchell had been appointed Ryder's personal golf tutor a few years earlier at the remarkable fee of £1,000 per annum.

A rare snapshot of Bobby Jones reporting on the Ryder Cup action at Columbus, Ohio, 1931. Despite having won numerous major titles, the American golfing legend was never eligible for the Ryder Cup because he was an amateur.

American professionals, Al and Abe
Espinosa pose with Densmore Shute
(centre) in a publicity photograph for
the 1931 Ryder Cup at Scioto Country
Club, Ohio. While Abe (right) never
actually played in the match, he was
there to cheer his brother on to victory
against English professional Ernie
Whitcombe in the singles.

Walter Hagen during his humiliating 10&8
defeat by George Duncan in the Ryder
Cup at Moortown, 1933.

With Sam Ryder looking on, two rival captains – J.H. Taylor (left) and Walter Hagen (right) – greet each other during the opening ceremony of the 1933 Ryder Cup match at Southport and Ainsdale. While it is smiles all round for the cameras, the two men apparently disliked each other with a passion. While Taylor considered American captain Hagen too flamboyant for his tastes, Hagen thought Taylor was old-fashioned. Their relationship was certainly not enhanced when Hagen almost struck Taylor the following day while practice swinging on the first tee.

Abe Mitchell hitting his opening tee-shot at the short first in the 1933 Ryder Cup at Southport and Ainsdale. The board to the right shows this was match two of the final day singles, with the English professional going on to defeat American Olin Dutra by the embarrassing margin of 9&8. It was a good day all round, as the British side went on to beat the USA by a single point to record their second victory in the event.

Having led his USA Ryder Cup side to victory at Southport in 1937, Walter Hagen takes a well-earned break in Scotland. A keen huntsman, he rarely missed the opportunity to fish or shoot when overseas.

The 1947 British Ryder Cup team arrive in Chicago shortly before the match at Portland and are presented with the key to the city. Back row, left to right: Robert Hudson (sponsor of the event), Arthur Lees, Eric Green, Max Faulkner, Henry Cotton, Jimmy Adams, Sam King and R.C.T. Roe (secretary of the PGA). Front row: Reg Horne, Charlie Ward, Fred Daly and Dai Rees.

Henry Cotton showing a typically well-balanced
follow through in the Ryder Cup at Portland,
Oregon, 1947.

Max Faulkner entertains his fellow professionals by mimicking their golf swings during the Ryder Cup
at Ganton, 1949. While American captain Ben Hogan (centre) seems amused, British team member
Arthur Lees (second from right) obviously does not.

Ben Hogan and Dai Rees toasting each other with milk during the 1949 Ryder Cup at Ganton.

Ryder Cup team mates Max Faulkner and Harry Bradshaw discuss the latest golf equipment at Lindrick, 1957. A rare British victory, it would be the last for over twenty years.

Scottish professional Eric Brown contemplates his approach to the first during the 1957 Ryder Cup at Lindrick. Matched against the equally fiery Tommy Bolt in the singles, the match ended in defeat for the American by the margin of 4 & 3. As they shook hands, Bolt commented how little he had enjoyed the game. Typically, Brown replied in blunt style: 'No, neither would I if I had been given the hiding I just gave you!'

An unusual photograph from the 1973 Ryder Cup at Muirfield. A confident Lee Trevino (sitting) boasted he would 'kiss the American team's asses' unless he beat Peter Oosterhuis in the following day singles. The record shows he halved the match, and his team – including Jack Nicklaus and Arnold Palmer – are awaiting his unfulfilled promise!

The great American professional Arnold Palmer, pictured at Portmarnock in 1960.

CHAPTER SIX

FROM HICKORY TO STEEL: THE START OF THE MODERN ERA

In the fifty-year period from 1870 to 1920 golf evolved from a mainly Scottish pastime to a pre-eminent sport played all over the world. Over the years many theories have been offered as to why the game became so widespread in such a short time – including the expansion of the railways, the availability of cheaper equipment and the growing popularity of top name professionals. But while each had their effect, it was little compared to the impact made in the 1920s with the introduction of steel-shafted clubs.

Effectively ushering in the modern era, they literally revolutionised how golf was played. Before that the Royal and Ancient game was a relatively uncomplicated matter. Around the turn of the century golfers worked on the basis that if it worked, use it. Consequently inventors came up with all sorts of weird and wonderful ideas in the hope they would make them rich, including glass-headed putters, adjustable irons, metal woods, and even hippopotamus-faced wedges!

As for steel shafts, they had been a relatively old invention. As early as 1894 a blacksmith from Edinburgh called Thomas Horsburgh had tried to sell solid steel shafts to local professionals with little success. Whether they saw them as a threat to their trade in hickory shafts is unsure. What is certain is that after spending a small fortune developing his idea Horsburgh didn't live long enough to see his invention take off.

Almost three decades later a technical engineer named Saunders patented the first tubular steel shaft. But even with the backing of a leading golf company the idea was turned down flat by the R&A. With hickory shafts still in worldwide use, it was thought that golf would become too easy! Courses would have to have changed almost overnight to accommodate the fantastic distances ordinary golfers would now hit the ball. Of course this was never true, but at the time it was a genuine concern.

Despite this, steel shafts were in regular use in the United States by 1925. Helped by a worldwide shortage of hickory wood, the new clubs proved both popular and relatively inexpensive for the average American golfer. Deciding to legalise them the following year, the

Relics of a bygone era: a collection of ancient long nose woods, early blacksmith-made irons and feather-filled golf balls, photographed at St Andrews over a century ago.

USGA acted alone – unable to convince the R&A to agree. Attempts were made to win over the St Andrews club with little success. In Britain the PGA backed their decision, stating: 'the introduction of steel shafts would be detrimental to the professional trade in this country.'

It would be another three years before steel shafts were finally legalised in Britain. In that time the schism between the two governing bodies grew ever wider, and would never be truly healed again. Inevitably the sale of steel shafts grew in number, revolutionising the game on this side of the Atlantic as it had done in America. As for the humble club professional who thought his living would be threatened, extra production meant extra sales. Far easier to produce than hickory, matched sets of golf clubs became readily available to keep up with the increased demand.

Apart from the simple ability to hit the ball further, the introduction of steel shafts threatened the very courses that golf was played on. In London, for example, where space was increasingly restricted, established links like those at Tooting Bec and Clapham Common were gradually overwhelmed by the need for more land. Yet the change was far more fundamental than adding a few extra yards on to a hole.

In the United States the Gold Association which governed the game had already clashed with the R&A over the introduction of new technology. In 1910 the R&A outlawed the mallet-headed Schenectady putter which American Walter Travis had used to win both the

British and US Amateur Championships. Ruling that it departed from accepted guidelines of club design, a ban was made on the offending putter with immediate effect.

Inevitably, with tens of thousands of putters already in circulation in the United States, legal threats were made and a major crisis developed between the two organisations. Ultimately the R&A won, but it seemed to many that while the USGA were ready to embrace any innovation which made the game more pleasurable, the R&A steadfastly refused to sanction anything which departed from the norm. But the wind of change was blowing.

By 1923 a massive rebuilding programme was under way in Britain. Not only were the golf courses built in the late Victorian era being lengthened, but renewed interest in the game saw a massive growth in the actual number built. By the mid-1920s full-time golf course designers had sprung up all over Britain. Typical among these was the legendary Harry Shapland Colt. Former secretary at Sunningdale, he joined other designers like John Abercrombie, Herbert Fowler and Fred Hawtree in making a respected profession out of the designing and building of golf courses.

In the United States one of Colt's former associates, Alister MacKenzie, was in the forefront of golf course design. Like Colt, he had relinquished his former profession and had achieved some remarkable results. In the late '20s he took over the design of the now world-famous Cypress Point golf links on the Monterey Peninsular. Then, on the strength of this work, he was invited by Bobby Jones to help build his 'dream' course at Augusta National in 1931.

Back in Britain, the period immediately before and after the Second World War was also a time of considerable change. Social attitudes toward the humble golf professional had been lukewarm since the days of Vardon, Braid and Taylor, but with the advent of public school-educated players like Henry Cotton in the late '30s things slowly began to improve.

After the war, the PGA came under the able command of retired naval officer, R.C.T. Roe. While a full tournament schedule was still many years away, he encouraged exhibition matches between top players for charitable causes like the Red Cross. With players like Max Faulkner and Dai Rees taking part, they proved extremely popular in the late 1940s and '50s and helped to raise the public profile of golf pro's in general. After a decade of turmoil, the game of golf had survived, and now looked forward to the future with renewed zeal.

As for the hickory shaft, that was now as much a part of golfing history as the feathery ball and long-nose wood.

Tom Williamson (centre) and his staff at Notts Golf Club, 1889. Williamson having joined the club only two years earlier, this photograph was intended to show the members just how well organised his business was.

The finishing shop at Gibson's of Kinghorn, c. 1898. Shortly before the club heads were fitted with a hickory shaft, they were given a thorough polishing before being stamped with the company's name. The photograph shows workmen in the process of 'finishing them off', while the different grades of wire rag sit on the benches behind them.

An effective turn-of-the-century advert for the Silvertown golf ball.

Tom Dunn (1849–1902) was a former club maker, then golf course designer. Among the first to go full time from his offices at Meyrick Park Golf Club in Bournemouth, he was responsible for the construction of over 132 courses world wide.

Golfers playing from the 'Pulpit' tee at Aberdovey, 1898.

A tricky tee-shot at Aberdovey in Wales, 1898.

In the time when the British Amateur Championship was considered the equal of the Open, these golfers dominated the early years of the event, winning eight from the first nine. From left to right: Horace Hutchinson, John Ball junior and John E. Laidlay.

British Prime Minister Arthur Balfour standing outside the door of his country retreat, Chequers. A talented golfer in his youth, his enthusiasm for the game contributed more to its popularity in the early 1900s than anything else. In a newspaper report in 1899 he was described as 'extremely keen' on the game, while 'his desire to win is unflagging and his geniality is never ruffled no matter how dark the prospect may appear against him or his partner'.

In the early 1900s, long before computer-designed golf courses and mechanical diggers, greens like this one at Rickmansworth were built using horse-drawn scrapers to contour the land.

Taken during the construction of St George's Hill Golf Club in Surrey in 1911, this photograph shows the laborious way in which the fairways were seeded.

Former secretary of Sunningdale and premier golf course architect of the 1920s, Shapland Colt.

Donald Ross, legendary golf course designer.

The Prince of Wales selects a club on the third tee at Coombe Hill Golf Club in Surrey, 1921. Accompanied by his brother, the Duke of York, they were regular visitors to the club where they both took lessons from well-known Scottish professional Alex Herd (far left). Describing the Prince of Wales' golf clubs, Herd wrote later: 'I noticed that his "bag o' sticks" was a miscellaneous lot, bearing the names of several makers, showing that he had been patronising professionals in different parts of the country – one of the drawbacks of being a Prince! After all, makers like to be represented in the royal bag.'

More like a moonscape than a golf course. This shows the work that went on building Moor Park at Rickmansworth, designed by Harry Colt, in 1923.

George, Duke of York (later to become King George V) hits the opening drive at Richmond Park Golf Club attended by five-time Open Champion J.H. Taylor (far left), 1923.

Golfing on the Continent. A bare-footed caddie accompanies two golfers at Knocke Zoute Golf Club in Belgium in the early '20s.

Rising British star Henry Cotton shows off his golf swing at Richmond, 1928.

Top British amateur Cyril Tolley drives off for the home side in the 1930 Walker Cup at Sandwich.

Large crowds gather for the Amateur Championship at Prestwick, 1934. This photograph shows the closing stages of the semi-final match between James Wallace of Scotland (centre) and George Dunlap of the United States.

'Miniature golf on board the steamer *Resolute*.' A pleasant enough image of golf, this photograph was included in a German holiday brochure for 1934, published by the Reich Committee for Tourist Traffic!

Dressed in his RAF uniform, Henry Cotton accompanies his wife Toots to a women's event in 1941.

Taken at his home in 1942, this rare photograph shows three-time Open Champion Henry Cotton on his way for a round of golf. No doubt petrol rationing had something to do with his mode of transport.

The legendary South African Bobby Locke competing in the Goodhall Round Robin Tournament at Wykagyl Country Club, USA, 1948.

A classic golfing portrait of HRH Edward, Duke of Windsor. A keen player throughout his life, he was photographed at his Paris home shortly after his 55th birthday in 1949. He was elected captain of the Royal and Ancient in 1922. It was dutifully noted that despite playing off 14 handicap when the picture was taken, he 'often played down to 12'.

The rugged splendour of Royal Portrush links in Northern Ireland. It was home to the 1951 Open Championship, which still remains the only occasion that golf's oldest major championship has been played outside mainland Britain.

Peter Thomson of Australia competing at Wentworth in the World Match Play, 1950s or 1960s.

CHAPTER SEVEN

THE WIDE WORLD OF GOLF

Hardly Tiger Woods, but one amateur puts his full weight behind a drive at Bulwell Forest Golf Club, 1900.

An unusual photograph of four Open Champions in a car. Taken in Aberlady in 1906, shortly before the Open at Muirfield, it shows James Braid (seated front right), Ted Ray (seated back left), J.H. Taylor (seated back right) and Harry Vardon (standing right). Interestingly, Braid suffered from acute motion sickness throughout his life and never actually owned a car!

Popular Scottish comic Neil Kenyon gets to grips with a tricky lie at Wembley Golf Links, 1912.

'The frustrations of employing a caddie.'

Five-time Open Champion James Braid takes part in a very unusual match at Sidcup, 1913. Setting out in the dark and finishing at around midnight, the only help he received was from a single flashlight. Remarkably the tall Scot still managed to break 80!

A rather unusual hazard. During the early years of the First World War the British Army used Sandy Lodge Golf Club in Hertfordshire as an artillery range. The photograph shows two young soldiers practising with a machine gun, while the green beyond still has its flagstick in place.

During the later years of the First World War injured soldiers were sent back to England to recover at Hatfield Hospital near London. With golf seen as a gentle recreation, a putting green was set up on the front lawn with occasional competitions being held. This rare photograph shows patients, nurses and visitors looking on while one such event gets underway. Note the person keeping score third from the right.

'Roll up, Roll up!' American trick-shot specialist Alex Morrison reveals a novel way of publicising his golfing stage show in New York, 1920. Having picked up the idea from watching Harry Houdini perform in similar style, Morrison would hit feather-light golf balls into the crowd while perched on top of a motor car.

Red Indians come to Sunningdale! This was arranged as a publicity photograph in the early '20s for a 'Wild West Show' playing in London; the squaw on the right reveals a remarkably good golf grip.

'Do You Golf?' A fascinating photographic postcard from the early 1920s.

Having hit the opening drive at Richmond Park Golf Club in 1925, the Duke of York presents a silver sovereign to the caddy who collected his ball, with J.H. Taylor looking on (far left). The state of the man's clothing perhaps indicates just how much it meant to him.

A young caddie enjoys his much-deserved lunch break, 1920s.

A rather unusual match. In 1926 American champion Gene Sarazen was challenged to an eighteen-hole match against a fly fisherman at Pine Valley. Sarazen was forced to hole out each putt, while the fisherman only had to cast his fly into a small white circle. The result of the match is not known.

As the popularity of golf increased in the United States throughout the '20s, publicity stunts like this became more commonplace.

Winston Churchill (centre) finding things a little heavy going during a game at Royal West Norfolk, 1928. A keen player in his younger years, he was once famously quoted as saying: 'Golf is a game whose aim is to hit a very small ball into an even smaller hole, with weapons singularly ill-designed for the purpose.'

Abe Mitchell showing how to escape one-handed from a bunker, 1929. A respected teacher and author of four books on the game, the English professional was Sam Ryder's personal tutor for many years.

An unusual photograph of top American amateur George Von Elm about to drive off the roof of the Savoy Hotel in London, 1930. Like the rest of the US Walker Cup side, Von Elm was staying in the hotel.

Australian Test cricketer Don Bradman gets in some golf practice at Margate during a break from the Ashes series of 1930.

'Zululand Golf.' Taken in 1933 and later published in postcard format, this remarkable photograph has been subtly altered to make the walking sticks held by the natives look like golf clubs!

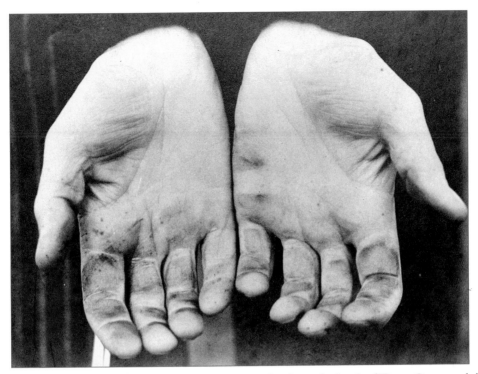

Taken during practice for the 1937 Open at Carnoustie, this shows the hands of Henry Cotton and the place where the actual club rested.

In 1940 golfers at Southend-on-Sea were advised to carry rifles with them during a round of golf, in case German paratroopers landed on the fairways.

This photo shows Arnold Palmer giving a chimp a golf lesson while a bemused Bob Hope looks on, 1960.

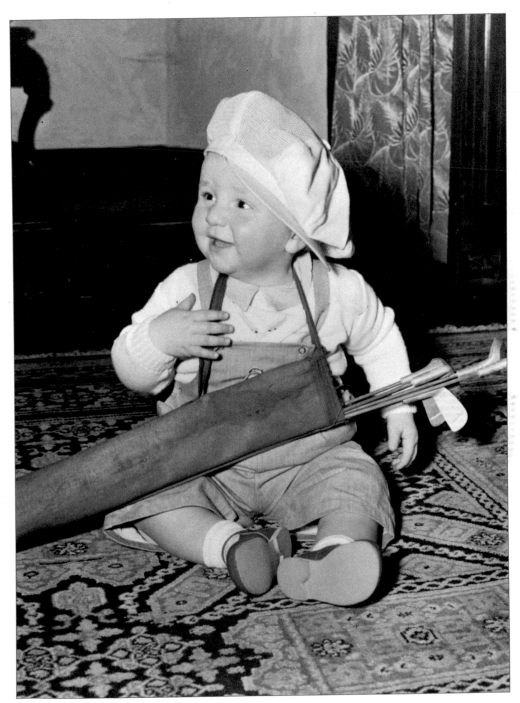

'You can never start playing golf too soon.'

ACKNOWLEDGEMENTS

Apart from a small number of golfing memorabilia images provided by Phillips of Chester, all photographs published in this book have come from the private collection of author Dale Concannon. As they represent the work of many photographers, known and unknown, it has not always been possible to ascertain the copyright holder – original or otherwise. Therefore it is humbly hoped that any such omission will be excused.

For further information about the Concannon Golf History Collection please direct enquiries to:

The Phil Sheldon Golf Picture Library
40 Manor Road
Barnet
Hertfordshire
EN5 2JQ

Tel: 0181 440 1986
Fax: 0181 440 9348